Sellout

Musings from Uncle Tom's Porch

By
Ron Miller

This book is dedicated to my grandfather, Melvin Lubin, who blessed me with his devotion to Jesus Christ, his passion for politics and, most of all, his love; and to Gary Mullen, dear friend, small group leader, elder, a man after God's own heart and everything that is good and right about America. May they rest forever in the loving arms of Jesus.

Table of Contents

Acknowledgements

I've been a writer since my high school days at Torrejon Air Base in Spain and Abilene, Texas. My essays about America won three national awards from the Freedoms Foundation at Valley Forge: the George Washington Honor Medal in 1976, the Defender of Freedom Award in 1977 and the Valley Forge Honor Certificate in 1978.

In 1978 I was hired as a researcher and speechwriter for A.L. "Dusty" Rhodes, a conservative Texas Democrat who ran for the U.S. House of Representatives, but lost the primary.

Nevertheless, that didn't stop me. I was a regular contributor to the op-ed section of my local paper and, once I arrived at Texas Tech University, I was the unofficial scribe for the College Republicans, where my op-eds in the campus paper generated days of discussion and debate.

In the Air Force, I applied my writing talents to the preparation of intelligence estimates, briefings to senior officers and operations plans, and some of my documents were being referenced years after I'd written them. In 1990, I even found time to write a paper in collaboration with an equally politically-minded friend, Mark Solomon. *Washington Post* syndicated columnist David Broder hailed it as "exceptionally clear and compelling"— more on the paper later.

Since then, I've written hundreds of plans, presentations, op-eds and online articles. Now, in this age of blogging and social networking, I've built up a devoted following around the country.

Despite my skills and production as a writer, it never occurred to me to write a book. Rather, it took some observant and assertive people in my life to move me in that direction. I owe them my heartfelt thanks.

Bill Cooper, my best friend and "brother from another mother," always used to say I had a book in me and he's always been one of my biggest fans.

Lee Ann Stedman made me believe it was actually feasible for me to write a book. She pointed out that I'd produced enough material already for several books and that I should pick a topic about which I was passionate and go deeper, using articles I'd already written as a jumping-off point.

Two years ago, Lori Roman invited me to join her in a venture called Regular Folks United and, not only has it changed my life, it gave me a dear friend and a partner in promoting liberty. She has been an unconditional and unabashed promoter and supporter of just about everything I do. I couldn't ask for a better friend.

Susan Carleson, president of the American Civil Rights Union, provided the resources we needed to secure a publisher, and you wouldn't be holding this book in your hands were it not for her.

Ken Blackwell and Niger Innis are stalwarts in the black conservative community, and I consider it a high honor to have them endorse my book.

I've had some amazing pastors and spiritual leaders in my life. Ever since I returned to the church in 1993, these men have helped me stay on the straight and narrow path and keep me focused on Christ, Who is ever on my mind and in my heart. Mark Ragsdale, Tony Montague, Michael Hailey and Robert Hahn are anointed by God and I am grateful that He brought them into my life.

Chesapeake Church has been "a place of grace" for me and my family. I cannot imagine enduring tough times or celebrating triumphs without my church family to love us and care for us.

Even when I screwed up, my mother and father always believed I had greatness in me. While my parents don't share my devotion to conservatism or my affiliation with the Republican Party, I daresay every child should have parents who are as affirming and supportive as mine.

A successful book project requires many eyes to ensure quality. Anna Womack reviewed an early draft to start me on my way, and I spent many days and nights with my editor and contributor, Anita Crane, polishing the book to a fine sheen. I'm pleased to say that the process resulted not only in a solid manuscript, but a friendship that I hope will last forever.

No family man can write a book without his loved ones giving up their time. My wife of 26 years, Annik, and my children, Amanda, Briana and Colin, let me vegetate in front of my computer screen, they tolerated me when I went web-surfing to clear my mind or when I had writer's block, and they let me believe that this could be a big deal. I married above my station and ended up with some great kids. In other words, it seems my family's goodness has more to do with them and God than it does with me.

Saving the best for last, I give thanks and praise to my Lord and Savior, Jesus Christ, the giver of all good things, the one Who gives me purpose in this life and hope for the next. I am sold out only to Him.

1

'A Nation of Cowards'

*"Though this nation has proudly thought of itself
as an ethnic melting pot, in things racial we
have always been and continue to be, in too
many ways, essentially a nation of cowards."*
~ Eric Holder, U.S. Attorney General

"A nation of cowards." Pretty harsh words coming from our newly confirmed attorney general, not yet one month removed from the inauguration of the first black president of the United States. Holder, himself a symbol of achievement as the first black to serve as the nation's chief law enforcement officer, was commemorating Black History Month by criticizing our inability, individually and collectively, to speak frankly on matters of race. Such a dialogue, he opined, is the only "way we can hasten the day when we truly become one America."

Mr. Holder took a lot of heat for his comments and I was one of those bringing the heat:

> [I]f we are a nation of cowards, Mr. Holder, it's
> because the black community doesn't encourage
> honesty but rather demands fealty to one world-
> view. If you want to eradicate cowardice in the
> national discussion on race, how about starting
> with us?

My beef with him wasn't with the intent of his statement—I, too, welcome the day when we can be honest with each other about race without incurring each other's wrath. The problems we have with, and perceptions we have of, one another can't be addressed if we are guarded in our disclosures and refuse to show our hand.

No, my objection was and is to the likely outcome of any attempts to discuss race honestly, especially in the black community. Let's be blunt: The white community isn't going to talk about race in any form or fashion because they don't want to be labeled as racists. It's like inviting them to walk through a minefield. The chances of their getting to the other side unscathed are practically nil.

Black people who wish to have an honest dialogue about race in America aren't treated any better. Ask Bill Cosby what happens when he speaks frankly about race and class to his fellow black Americans. Talk to Shelby Steele, John McWhorter, Thomas Sowell, Joseph C. Phillips, Star Parker, Ken Blackwell, Roy and Niger Innis, LaShawn Barber, Justice Clarence Thomas or any other black person who has dared to be candid about his or her views on race in America.

Not only will the high priests and scribes of the black orthodoxy lay waste to our reputations and integrity, they will sanction sympathetic whites to do the same. Oh, and no epithet is off limits, even if it is racially charged. The white enablers of the black orthodoxy are almost giddy with glee as they practice their best racist statements against those black men and women who dare to offer an opinion on race that deviates from the politically correct rendition of the state of blacks in America today.

I know this firsthand because I am a "sellout"—a Sambo, a Stepin Fetchit, a house Negro, an Uncle Tom. I know it because I refuse to become one with the hive and

I am protective of the individuality and independence bestowed upon me by the Creator.

Incidentally, those who use the phrase "Uncle Tom" as a slur have no concept whatsoever of the character in Harriet Beecher Stowe's famous anti-slavery novel, *Uncle Tom's Cabin*. Tom was a noble Christian man who endured the hardships of enslavement with amazing grace. He refused an order from Simon Legree, his cruel white master, to whip a fellow slave and was savagely beaten by Legree as a result. He also heroically resisted Legree's attempts to break him of his faith in Christ.

Tom comforted the other slaves, encouraged two of them to escape and refused to divulge their whereabouts to Legree. Because of this, he was beaten to death by two black slaves, Sambo and Quimbo, who acted as Legree's overseers. Tom forgave his assailants even as he was dying and they were so humbled by his mercy that they became Christians too. So Stowe's main character is a man of great dignity and Christian faith.

Tom represented Stowe's deliberate attempt to dispel the popular minstrel show stereotypes of black men as ignorant, lazy and frolicsome buffoons. In fact, it was the minstrel shows that subsequently took the Uncle Tom character and twisted him into a happy-go-lucky, boot-licking apologist for his white masters.

It seems that neither the minstrels nor the audiences of Stowe's day were ready to accept the portrayal of a black man as better than a white man, no matter how evil the villain was. So in contempt for Tom's goodness, many of the minstrel shows disposed of Simon Legree altogether.

Nonetheless, I smile when I'm called an Uncle Tom because, in the character's original and intended incarnation, he is a Christ-like figure. My willingness to embrace what my adversaries think is an insult confounds them, which brings me even more pleasure.

The reason we are "a nation of cowards" when it comes to discussing race is because we don't permit honesty to enter into the dialogue. There is a prescribed narrative that is deemed acceptable and no deviations from that narrative are permitted without negative consequences.

Yet I am no coward. Anyone who reads my articles on the internet—or anyone who's read one of my letters to the editor of my local newspaper—can vouch for my fearlessness in discussing and debating issues of race or any topic related to politics, society and faith.

There's an old saying that goes "Never discuss religion or politics in polite company." Well, I broke that rule a long time ago and we may as well add race to the list because the response of "polite company" to that topic is likely to be equally charged as it would be to the first two.

So let's talk about race in America, but from the perspective of a proud Uncle Tom and sellout. You may not like or accept what I have to say, but I am certain of my right to say it because it's not a privilege to be granted or revoked by the black orthodoxy, their white enablers or anyone else. I was conceived in the image of God, "fearfully and wonderfully made."[a] I am a free man in the Creator's universe with a view of the world that is uniquely mine and mine to express as I think best.

Jesus Christ says, "[Y]ou will know the truth, and the truth will make you free."[b] I didn't fully grasp what that meant until after more than 50 years of living. The knowledge of the truth instills in a person clarity, confidence and serenity, allowing one to stand firm against the lies and attacks of the world without fear.

Courage is true freedom and I came to that place because of Jesus Christ. Only in Him, the Eternal Word and Truth Incarnate, am I free to be a contrarian black man.

---

[a] Psalm 139:14.

[b] John 8:32.

2

A Different Road

*"Two roads diverged in a wood, and I–
I took the one less traveled by,
And that has made all the difference."*
~ Robert Frost

My first fight took place in 1959 at Lake Charles Memorial Hospital in Lake Charles, Louisiana, where my maternal grandmother worked in the laundry room. As my mother likes to recall, I was so small at birth and so sick that the doctors were convinced I wasn't going to live. Born at 2 pounds 7 ounces, all I could do was accept it as my fighting weight.

The doctors tried to have me transferred to the local charity hospital because they didn't think my parents had the means to pay for the expensive care my condition required. My father, however, was an airman stationed at nearby Chenault Air Force Base and the U.S. Air Force covered my treatment at Lake Charles Memorial, ensuring that I got the best care in the region.

Even with that, the doctor attending to me declared I wouldn't survive the night.

My relatives love to tell the story of how, following the doctor's prognosis, they all went to the hospital chapel to pray overnight. By morning, the doctor was amazed to see me still alive. I had some rough months ahead and more than a few visits to the hospital, but I pulled through. The elders in my family always told this story to me as evidence that God had something great planned for me, and this instilled in me a desire to discover and fulfill God's plan for my life.

I'm not sure if it was my frail health, the doctor's prediction that I would be "slow" because of the travails of my early life, my mother's protectiveness or some combination of the three, but I grew up spending a lot of time indoors reading. My favorites were a collection of classic children's stories, the Encyclopedia Britannica and a science reference set. I remember reading early and often, which led me to a fondness for good writing and a fairy tale view of life inspired by the tales of Camelot, the Arabian Nights, and the Brothers Grimm.

As the first child and grandchild, I never lacked for attention. My parents encouraged my interest in reading and learning. Actually, I was spoiled by my grandparents, especially my maternal grandfather. He was friendly, well-liked and respected by everyone I knew— and he loved children, especially his grandchildren.

He was a deeply religious man who served as a deacon at Mount Calvary Baptist Church and often led the prayer during the lengthy and hot Sunday services. I credit his example and spiritual instruction as the primary influence in my decision to accept Christ at the age of nine and be baptized at the church where he served and my mother grew up.

My grandfather visited us in Idaho one summer and was pleased to see my devotion to Christianity and my interest in politics, for these were his passions as well. I thought I'd grow up to be a politician or a preacher or some combination of the two, either a socially active pastor or a faith-based public servant.

As I witness the endless debates today about the role of religion in the public square, I think back to the summer of 1969 in Idaho and how I saw no conflict whatsoever between serving Christ and serving people in the political arena. Both roles require service before self and a genuine regard for people as equal heirs, whose value and dignity are intrinsic to their very humanity. It is impossible to separate the unalienable rights stated in the Declaration of Independence from their foundation in the Judeo-Christian belief that we are all equal in the sight of God.

While I shared my grandfather's faith and passion for politics, I didn't inherit or take interest in his skills as a laborer. He was a man who worked with his hands all his life: at the petrochemical plant where he made his living, at home on his cars and trucks, and on the many old homes he purchased, refurbished and rented out to people in the neighborhood.

While he always expressed pride in my academic achievements, he never fully understood my "book learning" as he called it. He would tease me over my mannerisms and diction, sometimes calling me "a white cake with chocolate frosting" who "talked propah," as he and other relatives of mine would say.

Nonetheless, I adored my grandfather growing up and during our occasional stops in Lake Charles between my father's Air Force duty assignments, I looked forward to being around him and currying his favor.

Things became interesting one day during a visit from college when I announced to my family that I was registering as a Republican. Like most black families, they believed the Democrats were "for" black people and Republicans "against" us. Therefore, they aligned with the Democrats. The fact that practically all the discrimination inflicted upon them in their lifetimes came at the hands of Democrats didn't seem to matter.

I didn't know any better growing up, but once I left the house and started to draw my own conclusions about life, a lot of what I thought I knew didn't add up. For starters, I learned the Republicans had over a century of commitment and accomplishment in the name of equal rights for blacks, while it was the Democrats who came late and reluctantly to the party.

History shows it was the Democrats who fought to keep slavery, instituted Jim Crow laws, established the Ku Klux Klan, lynched thousands of blacks, emasculated our men and abused our women, and resisted every civil rights bill or constitutional amendment in Congress, even the landmark Civil Rights Act of 1964, right up to the mid-1960s. Civil rights legislation passed only because Republicans supported it.

President John F. Kennedy, whom most blacks revere, was indifferent to Dr. King and the civil rights movement. As a senator, he voted against the 1957 Civil Rights Act and, as president, he had to be persuaded to allow the 1963 March on Washington during which Dr. King gave his famous "I Have a Dream" speech. He saw the civil rights movement as a distraction and its leaders as agitators. For example, he accused the Freedom Riders of being unpatriotic at a time when the nation was facing international crises involving the Soviet Union, Cuba and Vietnam.

Once on my own, I observed that the Republicans I met in college and in proximity to the university were kind and showed me a great deal of goodwill.

A roomful of almost exclusively white College Republicans from every corner of Texas elected me the state organization's executive vice chairman, even though I'd only been with my campus chapter for about three months and no one at the convention knew me at all before I launched my campaign. If they didn't like blacks, they had a funny way of showing it.

Throughout my life, practically every person I've met who is Republican or conservative has treated me with respect and grace, even love in many cases. They've been generous with their time, talent and treasure, and even helped me and my family during a rough period in our lives, with no expectation of reward or recognition. It was easy for me to let go of the stereotype the black community had of Republicans.

The other thing I discovered after I left home is that the values with which I was raised seemed more prevalent in the Republican Party platform.

My parents and grandparents instilled in me my faith in Jesus Christ, the discernment to know right from wrong, a sense of personal responsibility and accountability for my actions, a strong work ethic, and a drive for excellence over excuses in whatever I did.

My grandfather was an entrepreneur who taught himself to be a carpenter and electrician, and who purchased dilapidated homes, fixed them up and rented them out. Despite the fact he had only a sixth grade education, he made a very good life for his wife and two children.

My family is staunchly pro-life and often critical of people on welfare, most of whom they believe aren't at the end of their rope, but are simply lazy and abusing the system for their own benefit.

My family believes that government should uphold the law, but otherwise they don't need government in every aspect of their lives. We turn to family, church and community before we ever turn to government for help. Government is the refuge of last resort, not the first.

We believe sex is for marriage and that marriage is a lifetime covenant between a man and a woman for the raising of healthy, obedient, well-adjusted children.

My father's more than two decades of military service inspired me to pursue an Air Force commission as an air intelligence officer, and I served for over nine years, attaining the rank of captain. My experiences as a military dependent and a veteran instilled in me a great love for my country which has never diminished.

My grandfather owned several guns and would have taken aim at anyone who threatened to take them away.

In short, if you stripped away race, we would be considered a staunchly conservative family.

Ask most black conservatives how they arrived at the place they find themselves philosophically and I think they'll have a story similar to mine.

Many were raised in homes with conservative values but liberal allegiances. Only after they reached the age of discernment and started thinking with their heads rather than their hearts did they realize they were on the wrong side of the aisle.

I see in liberals a condescending paternalism toward blacks as if we are incapable of surviving and thriving on our own. The positions they take on several issues show utter contempt for God, the Bible and the values therein.

Liberals convey scorn for free markets, equality of opportunity and wealth. They are more interested in keeping us in a constant state of grievance and dependence on them, goading us into believing we must wring concessions out of a nation that has sinned, and must be punished in perpetuity for its transgressions.

At the time of decision, it didn't matter to me if these attitudes were the result of a calculated strategy to keep blacks beholden to them and their political ambitions, or a deeply held worldview. The cognitive dissonance between what I previously believed and what I observed with my own eyes was too great for me not to change.

My grandfather conceded that I'd probably get more visibility and attention as a black Republican. While that wasn't my motivation, I took his comment as a step in the right direction. I thought maybe if he gave me the chance, I could explain to him what I had learned.

That opportunity never came. He passed away unexpectedly in the fall of 1992 and I was devastated by his death. I had long since moved away and established a family of my own, so I was surprised by my own emotions. I was grateful he had a chance to come out and see me and my family just a few short months before.

My family and I were stationed in Florida and my grandfather decided out of the blue that he had to come and see us. He and other family members made the trek to our house, the first one we'd ever owned, and they spent a few days with us. It was a very pleasant visit and my grandfather realized that my "book learning" had led to a pretty good life for me and my family.

At one point during his visit, he asked me to ensure that my grandmother would be cared for after he was gone. He spoke about my responsibilities to the family as the oldest and most accomplished of his grandchildren. While I didn't understand why he felt the need to discuss these things with me at that time, I was grateful for his trust. Although we saw him once more before he died, it is that visit to Florida that I cherish the most.

For his funeral and burial, I traveled to Louisiana with my youngest daughter, Briana. As we flew over the southwestern Louisiana landscape on my way home and I looked out the window and down upon the swampy land to which we had just committed his body, I realized just how much of my grandfather was in me. The tears welled up in my eyes as I thought of how he made me the man I had become.

3

Renewing My Mind

*"And do not be conformed to this world,
but be transformed by the renewing
of your mind, so that you may prove
what the will of God is, that which
is good and acceptable and perfect."*
~ The Letter of Paul to the Romans, 12:2

My journey to faith and my conversion to conservatism went down separate paths but converged later in my life. To tell the truth, it is my full commitment and devotion to Christ that has strengthened my dedication to conservative principles and causes, a statement I'm sure rankles Christians who believe the worlds of faith and politics should be kept apart or that Jesus is a liberal and on their side rather than mine.

I mean no disrespect to anyone who believes in Christ but doesn't share my worldview. It's not my place to validate anyone's Christian walk and I hope no one seeks to cast aspersions on mine because I don't think or act as they do in the worldly realm of public policy. The union of faith and politics within me is unique to me and no one else has taken or ever will take my path. Yet as I chronicle my journey, I hope my logic will be apparent to you.

Just as my early political beliefs were influenced by my parents and grandparents, so was my faith. As I indicated previously, my grandfather was a primary influence in leading me to a profession of faith in Christ. My parents went to church on Sundays and spoke casually of Christ as a fact of life, but my grandfather was passionate about the Lord, and I was swept up in his ardor for Christ and the church. When I walked to the front of Mount Calvary Baptist Church to express my desire to be baptized, my grandfather was beaming and I was glad that he was pleased.

One of the more interesting aspects of my growing up in the church was that I didn't attend the same church throughout my childhood. In fact, my church "home" changed every time we moved with my father to his next duty station. The only church that was somewhat of a constant throughout my childhood was Mount Calvary, and then only between assignments or when my father was on a temporary tour of duty overseas and we couldn't accompany him.

You couldn't have asked for a greater contrast than the one that existed between Mount Calvary and the chapels we attended on military bases worldwide. The chapel services were no longer than an hour, tightly scripted and melded the denominations that weren't Catholic, Orthodox, Buddhist, Jewish, Mormon or Islamic into a single amalgam called "Protestant." The liturgies were staid and traditional, and the congregation quietly attentive—some called them "the frozen chosen." The chaplain was usually a white male and the majority of the congregants were white, but it didn't seem to be an issue for anyone in attendance, including my parents.

In my teen years, the chapels began hosting "Gospel" services patterned after the black churches, meaning the Christian churches that minister to predominantly black congregations in the United States. It was an attempt to appeal to black service members and their families, but I didn't go to any of them and, if my parents did, I wasn't aware of it.

When we were in Lake Charles, however, it was a whole different ball game. Mount Calvary was affiliated with the National Baptist Convention, one of the largest black denominations in the country, and it was one of the largest black churches in the city. It was rare to see a white face in the sanctuary and, when we did, it was usually a visiting dignitary, typically a politician seeking our favor. Decades later, I had my own personal experience with that particular ritual, but we'll get to that eventually.

While the chapel services were short and structured, Mount Calvary's services were two and a half to three hours long. And while there was an order of service, one could never predict when someone would "get happy," as in one or more members of the congregation, presumably overcome by the Holy Spirit, jumping to their feet, screaming and calling out the Lord's name, and flailing about while the ushers came to their aid, fanning them and restraining them from hurting themselves or others.

Being the quiet and self-contained child I was, I was always taken a little aback by these displays. I remember the first time I brought my new wife to a service at Mount Calvary and I cringed when someone in the congregation began to shriek and dance in the aisle. I wondered what she must think of all this carrying on. While she wasn't a regular churchgoer when we met, she'd been raised in the Catholic Church in France, and I knew their Masses were much more reserved. I confess I was embarrassed and didn't want her to think that was how I worshipped. Frankly, I wasn't doing much worshipping at that time in my life, but we'll get to that too.

These displays of emotion in church bothered me because the services I attended for most of my formative years were not nearly as demonstrative, so it was outside of the norm for me. I wondered whether it was right to call so much attention to oneself when we were supposed to be focused on God.

I also didn't believe the Holy Spirit would be possessing people in black churches but not white, so I questioned the legitimacy of most of these demonstrations. I hadn't heard of Pentecostal or charismatic churches at the time, so I admit I was wrong to think that way.

In fact, I was wrong about a lot of things related to church and worship, but it wasn't until I'd become more spiritually mature that I realized it and grew to respect the nature of the black church and other charismatic denominations.

As a mature Christian, I look forward to the worship in these congregations and it is revealing to see the creativity and energy in the body of Christ, especially in the black churches. I've seen more enthusiasm at a Washington Redskins football game than in some churches where we're supposed to be praising the Creator of the universe, so their unhindered worship is inspiring. At my home church, we say "Full devotion to God is normal" and the black churches get it.

Personally, I've grown to where I express myself by closing my eyes and lifting my hands to the Lord in reverence. I never would have done that in my younger years. Rather than viewing it as a way of calling attention to myself, I consider it a time of personal connection between me and the Lord.

My home church is non-denominational and brings together people from diverse backgrounds and religious experiences. All are welcome to come and worship in whatever fashion they wish. Some sit in quiet contemplation, some weep, another shouts out loud at the top of her lungs in a primal scream. It's a tribute to the intensely personal relationship that exists between a devout Christian and his or her Lord.

I lacked that personal relationship with Christ growing up, even though I consciously gave my life to

Him. The people I knew and trusted most believed in Him, so that was enough for me at the time.

In my teen years, church had become somewhat obligatory for my family and I was not immersed in Bible study or any other spiritual activity outside of the church walls on Sundays. It wasn't until I left home that I realized I had no anchor within my faith to help me stand firm when I was challenged by circumstances or others who didn't share my beliefs.

Discussing the necessity of Christian maturity, St. Paul states, "As a result, we are no longer to be children, tossed here and there by waves and carried about by every wind of doctrine, by the trickery of men, by craftiness in deceitful scheming."[c] Likewise, St. Peter admonishes us in saying, "[S]anctify Christ as Lord in your hearts, always being ready to make a defense to everyone who asks you to give an account for the hope that is in you, yet with gentleness and reverence."[d]

When I struck out on my own, I was still an infant spiritually and was ill-prepared to defend my beliefs in a world that was hostile to them. It wasn't long before I drifted away from the church and it was a thinly veiled racist statement from a black pastor at Mount Calvary that I seized upon as justification to put religion in my rear-view mirror. Going forward, I professed to believe, but I didn't practice my beliefs and I didn't go to church unless I was visiting my parents and they took us there.

My grandfather's unexpected death brought me back to Christ after more than 12 years of separation. Seeing him there in his coffin shook me to my core—the mannequin I gazed upon was not the man I knew. What happened to his smile, his joy for life, his love, his spirit? I couldn't accept the idea that the thoughts

---

[c] Ephesians 4:14.

[d] 1 Peter 3:15.

and emotions that made my grandfather alive to me had just dissipated like smoke. I knew in my heart they had to have gone somewhere. I returned to the faith of my youth to find my answers and then I sought to draw my own conclusions rather than accept what my parents and grandparents had told me.

I believe that when a human person genuinely opens himself to the possibility of God, He reveals Himself to that soul. I wanted to believe and He showed me the path back to faith. He knew exactly how to start me down that path—He appealed to my mind rather than my heart.

I believe people reach conclusions with either their heads or with their hearts, and where one leads, the other follows. I make decisions in my mind first and my heart then follows, so I have to be persuaded intellectually before I'm committed emotionally. Others are emotionally driven and they shape their thoughts to reinforce their feelings. Feelings, in my opinion, can betray you and much of Christian teaching encourages study, reflection and critical thinking to "be transformed by the renewing of your mind."[e]

For me, the evidence which brought about the renewing of my mind was the historicity of Jesus' resurrection from the dead. I concluded that if the resurrection really did happen, then everything changes and we cannot live our lives the same way. If it didn't happen, then nothing matters and we can live however we choose.

I concluded that the resurrection is a reality and the rest of the story fell into place for me. If Jesus rose from the dead just as He said He would, then not only did He keep His word and conquer death, something no other religious leader can claim, but it means He is who He said He is—the Son of God.

---

[e] Romans 12:2.

It also means that everything He said and taught was gospel, if you'll pardon the pun, and the correct response from me is to be obedient. I've strived to live a life of faithful service and devotion to Christ since then and I've never looked back nor regretted it.

All things considered, I no longer try to put God in a box and take Him out only at church on Sundays. The Creator of the universe is worthy of worship and praise all day, every day—and if He doesn't affect every aspect of my life, then I haven't surrendered to Him as my Lord and Savior. We can't claim to follow God and then refuse to obey Him.

The certainty with which I embraced Christ had an effect on my politics as well. While I was always more conservative politically than my black peers, my lack of bedrock principles had me drifting along the continuum from right to center. As I viewed the Word of God in a new light, it had an impact on every area of my life, including my political beliefs. The more I learn from the Bible, the more I learn from trusted spiritual mentors and teachers of the Word, the more I am convinced that my political principles have a bedrock solid foundation in the teaching and commands of Christ.

I know there are a lot of liberal readers who rose up out of their seats in objection to my previous statement. I'm not saying that God embraces conservatism. On the contrary, it's the other way around. I promise to expound upon my convictions in a later chapter and then you can reach your own conclusions.

As with my recommitment to my faith, I made the decision to become a conservative with my head rather than my heart. Sometimes I turn the tables on my parents and other black associates who question my conservatism and Republicanism. I simply ask them why they are Democrats.

The responses I get are generally emotional responses. "The Democrats have done more for blacks" or

"Republicans are greedy and selfish" or "Republicans hate blacks."

"Really?" I reply. "Do you have evidence to support those claims or are you just repeating what everyone else tells you?"

The Democrats declared war on poverty in 1964 and introduced us to the Great Society, a massive government entitlement program that was going to eradicate poverty in our lifetime, and which is often cited by blacks as evidence Democrats care more about them than Republicans.

According to the U.S. Census Bureau, in 1959 there were 39 million poor people in America. In 1964, it was 36 million. In 2004, 37 million. That's progress?

In fact, that's a very poor return on the $8-10 trillion we've spent on antipoverty programs since 1964. Blacks are three times more likely to be poor than whites, so where have these Democratic programs, however well-intentioned, led us?

In 1965, Daniel Patrick Moynihan released his report, *The Negro Family: The Case for National Action.* He revealed the rate of children being born out of wedlock in the black community was approaching crisis levels at 24% and that government antipoverty programs were, in effect, urging single women to have children and raise them in fatherless homes.

Moynihan declared, "At the heart of the deterioration of the fabric of Negro society is the deterioration of the Negro family. It is the fundamental source of the weakness of the Negro community at the present time." The study proposed that poorly designed government programs could destroy the black family.

Despite Moynihan's exhaustive research and detailed observations, blacks and liberals accused him of "blaming the victim" and giving comfort to racists. Still, his report proved to be prescient.

Today, 72% of all black children are born out of wed-lock and black single-parent homes are more likely to be trapped in a permanent underclass status. According to the most recent National Urban League report, *The State of Black America*,[f] blacks are twice as likely to be unemployed, three times more likely to live in poverty and more than six times as likely to be imprisoned compared with whites.

The black family wasn't always in peril, even in our worst years as a people in the U.S. In the years that followed slavery up until about 1925, five of six black children under the age of six lived with both parents. In the 1950s, the percentage of black children with both parents in the home was in the low-to-mid 80s. Despite the shadow of slavery, despite racial intimidation and the presence of institutionalized discrimination, black families stayed together.

The social upheaval of the 1960s rocked the institutions and values we once accepted as time-tested and proven, and which made our families strong—traditional marriage, which recognized the unique and complementary roles of a father and mother in raising children, the church as the moral compass of our communities and our nation, and personal responsibility and accountability for our behavior.

Today, not only are our families disintegrating, we are killing each other off. Department of Justice statistics show that between 1976 and 2005, 94% of blacks murdered in America were killed by other blacks. We have lost our respect for life and each other.

Liberal attempts to redefine marriage as something other than a lifetime covenant between a man and a woman for the purposes of raising a family have not helped the black family. Walter Fauntroy, a former District of Columbia non-voting delegate to Congress,

---

[f] March 24, 2010.

founding member of the Congressional Black Caucus and a coordinator for Martin Luther King, Jr.'s 1963 March on Washington, spoke eloquently of the consequences to the black community of redefining marriage:

Marriage is neither a conservative nor a liberal issue; it is a universal human institution, guaranteeing children fathers, and pointing men and women toward a special kind of socially as well as personally fruitful sexual relationship. Gay marriage is the final step down a long road America has already traveled toward deinstitutionalizing, denuding and privatizing marriage. It would set in legal stone some of the most destructive ideas of the sexual revolution: There are no differences between men and women that matter, marriage has nothing to do with procreation, children do not really need mothers and fathers, the diverse family forms adults choose are all equally good for children. What happens in my heart is that I know the difference. Don't confuse my people, who have been the victims of deliberate family destruction, by giving them another definition of marriage.

Then there is decriminalized abortion—that great moral stain on the American legacy which has resulted in the slaughter of some 50 million innocent and helpless children in the name of convenience. Black women make up 13% of the female population but account for 36% of all abortions. One out of every two black babies is aborted. Therefore, Reverend Clenard H. Childress, Jr. declared, "The most dangerous place for an African American to be is in the womb of their African American mother." More blacks have been killed by abortion since *Roe v. Wade* than all other causes of death combined. Every three days in America, the number of black babies killed by abortionists exceeds the number of blacks lynched between 1882 and 1968.

Planned Parenthood's role in this slaughter of black innocents is particularly troubling because the organization's founder, Margaret Sanger, was a known instigator of eugenics who called for a "pure" population through controlling the reproduction of "undesirable people." Her "Negro Project" was aimed at reducing the number of children born to American blacks because she viewed us as inferior. Therefore, she recruited the black church to bear the seeds of our own destruction:

> *We should hire three or four colored ministers, preferably with social-service backgrounds, and with engaging personalities. The most successful educational approach to the Negro is through a religious appeal. We do not want word to go out that we want to exterminate the Negro population and the minister is the man who can straighten out that idea if it ever occurs to any of their more rebellious members.*[g]

Sanger's legacy lives on in the Planned Parenthood Federation of America (PPFA) and the International Planned Parenthood Federation. PPFA places over 80% of its abortuaries in minority neighborhoods. Three summers ago, University of California at Los Angeles students conducted a sting on various Planned Parenthood facilities, thus exposing certain officials as all too eager to accept money from an avowed racist who insisted

---

[g] From a 1939 letter by Margaret Sanger to Dr. Clarence Gamble, heir to Proctor & Gamble's cofounder. Clarence used some of his fortune to fund 'birth control.' The original letter is owned by the Sophia Smith Collection, Smith College, Northampton, Massachusetts. The copyright to Margaret Sanger's papers at Smith College is co-owned by Alexander C. Sanger.

that his donation be used specifically to abort black babies.[1]

Back in 1966, prior to the transparency of the internet, Planned Parenthood gave Martin Luther King, Jr. its Margaret Sanger Award for his "resistance to bigotry" and, according to PPFA, it was accepted by his wife, Coretta Scott King. At that time, however, abortion was outlawed in most states, Planned Parenthood claimed opposition to abortion, and apparently Dr. King was unaware of Sanger's Negro Project.

Yet Alexander C. Sanger, Margaret's grandson, chair of the International Planned Parenthood Council, former "goodwill ambassador" for the United Nations Population Fund, and former president (1991-2000) of Planned Parenthood of New York City (PPNYC) and its Margaret Sanger Center International, is doing everything in his power to advance the racist agenda.

Upon taking the helm PPNYC, Alexander Sanger said, "With all her success, my grandmother left some unfinished business, and I intend to finish it."[2] He also said, "We currently have a small storefront office in central Harlem, and it is my first priority to see if we can transform that into a clinic."[h]

By 2005, the abortion industry's impact on New York City was so enormously tragic that *New York Magazine* dubbed the Big Apple "The Abortion Capital of America."[4] Moreover, as the writer points out, Planned Parenthood is the largest abortion chain there[h] and its Margret Sanger Center boasted about committing the most abortions.

Incidentally, President Obama's appointee, Secretary of State Hillary Rodham Clinton, received the 2009 Margaret Sanger Award.

---

[h] Planned Parenthood is also the largest abortion chain in the United States and the world.

Also in 2009, the *New York Times* conducted a revealing interview with Supreme Court Justice Ruth Bader Ginsburg. Discussing the court's majority opinion on *Roe v. Wade*, Ginsburg opined that her predecessors thought abortion would stunt the growth of "populations we don't want too many of." And that is a stunningly candid admission from a sitting member of the highest court in the land.

Likewise, in his 2005 book *Freakonomics: A Rogue Economist Explores the Hidden Side of Everything*, Steven D. Levitt made the controversial claim that 'legalized' abortion had led to a decrease in crime. Debates on his methodology, data and conclusions continue to this day, but he has not backed off from his claim or the rationale he used to justify it: the rationale that unwanted children are more likely to commit crimes than those who are wanted.

That rationale, however, has been sanitized for broader public consumption and his actual explanation for his theory is much more insidious. The book had been scrubbed of one particularly controversial statement related to his claim, a statement he made in a 1999 *Harvard Quarterly Journal of Economics* paper co-written with John J. Donohue:

> *Teenagers, unmarried women and African Americans are all substantially more likely to seek abortions. Children born to these mothers tend to be at higher risk for committing crime 17 years or so down the road, so abortion may reduce subsequent criminality through this selection effect.*

So the foundation of Levitt's argument is that decriminalized abortion reduced the crime rate by killing off the children of teenagers, singles and black women—because their children would have been predisposed to criminal behavior. Examination of these categories suggests that the predominant demographic group, whose termination purportedly contributed to a drop in the crime rate, is blacks.

Black women have the highest teen pregnancy rates in the nation, and since two-thirds of black children are born to single mothers, they tend to dominate in that category as well. We already know that black women account for a disproportionate number of all abortions.

The "selection effect" of which Levitt and Donohue so blithely speak is nothing more than eugenics, preventing the reproduction of "undesirables" by another name.

Eugenics and genocide may not be the stated policy of the abortionists, but in terms of action and outcome, they are fact. Population control, particularly among those who are perceived as a burden on society, is the DNA of abortion, so pro-abortion advocates can spare me the faux outrage over being called on it.

What infuriates me is our willingness to believe the most outlandish of conspiracy theories, like the levees in New Orleans being deliberately blown up after Hurricane Katrina to flood the black sections of the city or that AIDS was created in U.S. military laboratories to exterminate blacks. Yet we are presented with historical and empirical evidence of a sustained assault on the black community by the abortion industry, and we not only look the other way, we endorse it with our dollars and our votes. As a black conservative who has often been called "self-loathing," I contend that the majority of black Americans exhibit the epitome of self-loathing inasmuch as they are accessories to genocide. Furthermore, I refuse to be silent about it.

Today, black pastors like Reverends Jesse Jackson and Al Sharpton act as the "colored ministers" who lead the black population to embrace self destruction. They admonish other black pastors and congregations not to be misled by conservatives promoting the sanctity of human life or traditional marriage, despite all the evidence of the harm caused to the black community by their neglect or repudiation of those principles or institutions. They have abandoned their vows to the Lord for political glory here on earth.

One particular speech by Sharpton is very telling. Like all the Democratic presidential candidates in 2003, Sharpton was invited to campaign at a January 21st dinner given by the National Abortion Rights Action League, which was changing its name to NARAL Pro-Choice America in order to hide the deadly deeds that it pushes. There Sharpton said:

> *Let me say in all seriousness, as I came tonight I saw outside there are those that have chosen to picket this historic event. There is no question that of the six on this stage I have picketed more than any of them. [laughter]. I probably have picketed some of them. [laughter, applause].*
>
> *But I cannot remember a time that I have crossed a picket line. But tonight I proudly crossed that line. [applause]. As I crossed, a young lady said to me, "Forget your political activism, you're a minister and real Christians can't support that." And I said, "Young lady, it is time for the Christian Right to meet the right Christians." [cheers, applause]. "And not only the right Christians, but the right Jews and the right Buddhists and the right Muslims and the right atheists—people that believe in rights need to stand up and come together."[5]*

Indeed, all people who believe in human rights should stand together. But there is no right to abortion, so Sharpton's claim is an insult to God and the Gospel. "Rev." Sharpton and "Rev." Jackson grieve the heart of God for the sexual sins and murder they have excused and touted in His name.

Thankfully, many black ministers are leading a fledgling pro-life movement in the black community.

Alveda King, daughter of the late Rev. A.D. King and niece of Martin Luther King, is influential in her own right. After suffering post-abortion sorrow, she returned to God. Now this Dr. King leads several pro-life groups, and urges blacks to vote their values and support the fundamental right to life. She protested Obama's pro-abortion stance during his campaign, then his anti-life presidential policies.

Education is another arena in which Democratic liberal policies are failing black people. If a political movement could be sued for social malpractice, black Americans ought to be rushing to their nearest courtroom to indict liberals for condemning scores of young black males to lives of desperation and hopelessness. The symbiosis between the Democrats, local school boards and the teachers' unions has spawned an education bureaucracy that robs these young men of their future. While their actions are criminal, the tragedy is the apparent willingness of black people to enable this malpractice with their support or silence.

The plight of young black men has been a staple in the news but the statements bear repeating. In school districts across the nation, standardized test scores and high school grade point averages are consistently lower among black males compared to any other demographic group, even black females.

Only 47% of black males are graduating from high schools nationwide compared to 75% for white males.[6] In the state of Michigan, the black male graduation rate is an abysmal 33%.[7] The failure of more than half of young black males to earn a high school diploma has predictable and tragic consequences. These young men are more likely to be jobless, poor, engaged in criminal activity or incarcerated than their peers with diplomas.

The reasons behind these disparities could be argued endlessly. While we sit and squabble over why this is happening, another generation of young black men is consigned to a life of endless struggle. What I do know is there are educational alternatives demonstrating incredible success with young black men, and there are also enemies of these alternatives who are blindly beholden to a failed education bureaucracy at our children's expense.

Our inner cities provide the most egregious examples of how we're failing our young black men. The high school graduation rates in Detroit, Indianapolis and Cleveland are 24.9%, 30.5% and 34.1%, respectively.[8]

Yet in Milwaukee, which has had an alternative to public schools in place since the 1990s, 85% of students enrolled in the Milwaukee Parental Choice Program earned diplomas in 2007 compared to 58% in the Milwaukee public schools.[9]

There are other examples illustrating the success of educational alternatives in rescuing our young people. The Knowledge Is Power Program (KIPP), which runs 66 schools in 19 states and the District of Columbia, has had incredible success at raising reading and math scores among its overwhelmingly low-income and minority students, with math scores rising from the 41st to the 80th percentile, and reading scores from the 31st to the 58th percentile. Impressively, 85% of KIPP program participants go on to college.[10]

KIPP Houston High School graduated its first senior class the spring of 2009 and 96% of them were attending four-year colleges and universities in the fall.

In Maryland, Chesapeake Science Point Public Charter School outperformed Anne Arundel County public schools by up to 41% for black students on the Maryland State Assessment tests,[11] and their 7th and 8th graders scored 100% proficiency in beginning high school algebra compared to 63.5% in the state overall.[12]

Ask the parents of low-income minority children in Washington, DC about the benefits of parental choice. The DC Opportunity Scholarship Program provided $7,500 private school scholarships to poor children, most of them black or Hispanic, and the program has won praise from city leaders and parents alike for giving these children their first shot at a quality education.

Kevin P. Chavous, a former Washington, DC city council member and a national advocate and thought leader for parental choice, said, "This successful school voucher program—for DC's poorest families—has allowed more than 3,300 children to attend the best schools they have ever known."[13]

Moreover, a U.S. Department of Education evaluation revealed that these children are outperforming their peers in the DC public schools for about one-third of the cost.

As a result of these successes, black parents have been ardent supporters of parental choice for decades and some black elected officials are beginning to come around. In 2008, black Democratic state Sen. Ann Duplessis of Louisiana helped to pass a successful bill establishing a voucher program for low-income children. She declared, "We're... beginning to find out that the [public education] system doesn't work, a fact that's evident across the country. Instead of continuing to spend more money just repairing this old car, it's time to just buy a new one."[14]

The response of most Democratic politicians, school boards and teachers' unions to these impressive numbers and the widespread black endorsement of parental choice has not been laudatory. It has been harsh.

Democratic Party leaders in Congress and the Obama Administration have decided to end the DC Opportunity Scholarship Program, despite widespread support from DC government officials, the DC school chancellor and "more than 70% of DC residents."[15]

Mr. Chavous and the executive director of DC Parents for School Choice, Virginia Walden Ford, criticized the decision:

The decision to end the program, a decision buried in a thousand-page spending bill and announced right before the holidays, destroys the hopes and dreams of thousands of DC families. Parents and children have rallied countless times over the past year in support of reauthorization and in favor of strengthening the OSP.

Yet, despite the clearly positive results and the proven success of this program, Sen. Dick Durbin, Rep. Jose Serrano, Del. Eleanor Holmes Norton, and Secretary Arne Duncan worked together to kill the OSP. Funding the program only for existing children shrinks the program each year, compromises the federal evaluation of the program, denies entry to the siblings of existing participants, and punishes those children waiting in line by sentencing them to failing and often unsafe schools.

What is incredibly disappointing to low-income families in Washington, DC has been the silence of President Barack Obama. The President, who benefited from K-12 scholarships himself, worked on behalf of low-income families in Chicago, and exercises school choice as a parent, has stood silently on the sidelines while his Secretary of Education belittled the importance of helping such a small number of children in the nation's capital.[16]

Chavous and Ford demanded that President Obama and Congress come to the rescue "of low-income families in Washington, DC who deserve access to a quality education right now—not five years from now—but right now. These children deserve that opportunity."

Charter schools are supposed to have autonomy from the public school system so they can develop innovative programs to teach our children. Local school boards, however, have used laws and ordinances to keep charter schools from obtaining the facilities they need to operate or using school buses for transportation.

Since charter school funding in many states is funneled through the local school board, they've used that power to withhold funds and force some charter schools to close. If the bureaucracy doesn't work, lawsuits, rumor, intimidation and false accusations have been employed to discredit charter schools and their employees.

Why the hostility from institutions supposedly dedicated to excellence in education?

According to Pournelle's Iron Law of Bureaucracy, a pearl of wisdom from science fiction writer Jerry Pournelle, the people devoted to a bureaucracy eventually take control from those devoted to the goals the bureaucracy is supposed to accomplish.

The school boards and teachers' unions' primary goal is self-preservation, not education. Moreover, their embrace of liberal causes such as same-sex marriage indicates they have an agenda that goes beyond teaching our children to read, write and calculate. Charter schools and other parental choice options don't give them the opportunity to indoctrinate our children and teach them values without parental knowledge or consent.

Frustratingly, black parents continue to elect the same people who are determined to take away options to better educate their children. Black parents are overwhelmingly in favor of parental choice but don't realize the Democrats and their sycophants in the education bureaucracy hate parental choice and are the very reason their children are doomed to failing schools and less abundant lives.

Finally, Democratic economic policies are negatively affecting wealth creation in the black community, which is moving from consumption to the nascent stages of wealth building. The need is urgent: The net worth of blacks in America is only 1.2% of the total, a figure that hasn't changed since the end of the Civil War.

Black home and business ownership are at an all-time high and we have a real prospect of building generational wealth that we can pass on to our heirs.

Black entrepreneurs want to see the estate tax, also known as "the death tax," eliminated. They also want government paperwork reduced because both of these impositions have a disproportionate impact on minority businesses.

Who imposes these burdens on them? Tax-happy, regulation-obsessed liberal Democrats that get elected with their votes.

A most telling illustration of the dichotomy between black values and the people they elect is the outcome of several ballot initiatives during the 2008 general election.

Nationwide, 95% of black voters helped to elect President Obama. Still, 70% of black voters in California helped to pass a state traditional marriage amendment and 71% of black voters in Florida did the same. The majority of black voters in California also supported parental notification on abortion, although that measure failed to pass.

At the end of the day, given the preponderance of the evidence, I continue to ask myself, "Why are black people Democrats?"

It doesn't make sense in my head, given what we profess to believe and what the Democrats promote as policy. Democrats pass a lot of laws and establish a lot of programs, hopeful that something will stick, to show they care about blacks. The results, however, are disastrous.

Democrats are terrified of too many blacks processing the information in their heads just as I did and allowing their minds to lead them rather than their hearts. That is why they are quick to tag conservatives and Republicans as racists. They want to keep us frightened, angry and dependent. They know that if just 25-30% of blacks consistently voted Republican, the Democrats would never win a nationwide election again.

We desperately need to rebuild the foundations of our communities and live our values in all that we do. In our toughest times, we relied on our families, our communities and our faith to sustain us. Government assistance is an ineffective and wholly inadequate substitute for a father and mother in the home, a neighbor next door with a helping hand, or the church down the block.

The black church, in fact, wields a great deal of influence and shares a lot of the blame as well for where we are today. It is there that the collective renewing of minds in the black community can and should begin.

-4-

My Skinfolk Ain't Necessarily My Kinfolk

"But I figure if the king tells you to go conquer the hinterlands one day, and tells you to shoe his horse the next day, you should do them both without slacking. He is the king."
~ Andrée Seu

In 2006, I sought election to Congress and then the Maryland Senate, respectively. I'll share more with you later, but here I confess that one campaign ritual I dreaded was the obligatory church visit. I looked forward to the worship and the black churches I visited generally saw no conflict in blending faith and social responsibility.

While American society, including some mainstream churches, are doing everything they can to squeeze the last vestiges of faith from our culture, the black community understands that a faith which only manifests itself inside a church building on Sunday is useless and we don't serve a useless God. The black church's role as the center of the community, combined with Christ's command to be salt and light in the world, created a religious movement that was dedicated to mobilizing the faithful inside the church to take action outside the church.

So why my dread? For one thing, I was self-conscious about the stares of the congregation, many of whom I'm sure saw me as a heathen who was only setting foot in their church to seek their favor and win their votes. I understand how they feel. I'm leery of politicians who try to ingratiate themselves with the churchgoing community when it's clear they probably dusted off their Bibles just that morning. They stumble over Scripture and embarrass themselves in front of the congregation they're trying to impress. That isn't me, but they had no way of knowing how committed I am to Christ, that I'm active in ministry at my home church, that I was in fact one of them.

The other reason for my trepidation is political. Bluntly put, the black church may consider me a brother in Christ but because I am a Republican, I am not a brother in politics. As a result, I approached the entrance to every black church with apprehension, not sure what to expect. My colleague, another black Republican, and I were generally well received, but we had our moments.

At one church service, a man confronted us and essentially declared us fools for being aligned with the same political party as President George W. Bush. A spirited discussion ensued and my colleague eventually pulled me away because it was clear I wasn't going to convince this gentleman that my reasons for being a Republican were more valid than his reasons for being a Democrat.

Given the opportunity, I would have told him the only thing the Democrats do for us is keep race at the forefront of our minds and promote race-based policies which stroke our egos but really don't make our lives better. I would have criticized the fact that 90% or more of black citizens vote for the Democrats despite their decades of failure in making our schools better, our streets safer, and our families stronger and more self-sufficient. Further, I would have pointed out that we misinterpret Democrats' actions as caring, but they're really just keeping us angry and frozen in time so we'll continue to keep them in power. I didn't get the chance and it's probably just as well that I didn't.

At another church, a dapper young pastor with a degree from Harvard Divinity School welcomed us and another candidate into his study for introductions prior to the sermon. But once he stepped up to the pulpit, he delivered a diatribe blasting conservative evangelicals and the policies of the Bush Administration. I thought I was at a political demonstration and not a church service, so my heart hardened. I went to his church to worship, but I left unfulfilled and angry.

Later in the campaign season, I read in the news that this young pastor was in the hot seat for potentially crossing the line and endorsing a Democrat by attacking his Republican opponent, a black man. "Your skinfolk ain't necessarily your kinfolk," he declared, borrowing a line from black author Zora Neal Hurston which was popularized by NAACP president Julian Bond.

Ironically, Ms. Hurston was a prominent black libertarian and self-help advocate who used this line to criticize her black colleagues for their flirtations with leftist and Communist ideologies. She would have rejected this young pastor's apparent political leanings and Julian Bond's as well.

The pastor used a Biblical account of Jesus' trial at the hands of Pontius Pilate to further bring home his point, referring to people supposedly deceived into supporting the black Republican as "Barablicans" (read: Barabbas) and those who voted for the Democrat as "Jesuscrats." I'm sure Christ didn't approve of His name being abused by someone who declares himself a teacher of the Gospel.

That's not the first time a black pastor chose the world over his calling to preach the Word. The Reverends Jesse Jackson and Al Sharpton long ago abandoned being spiritual leaders and teachers, and exchanged the moral high ground for political advancement and worldly power.

My frustration with them has everything to do with the "Rev." prefix they carry. That designation bears with it a sacred obligation to uphold God's commandments and lead by example. Yet in at least one of their many campaigns against a perceived socio-political problem, they violated that obligation by essentially telling their 'flocks' to ignore the Word of God.

Prior to the 2006 elections, the reverends were alarmed at the trends they'd been seeing in places like Ohio, a battleground state crucial to President Bush's re-election in 2004. One of the interesting and critical sidebars to his Ohio victory was the increased percentage of the black vote he received there. When a Republican's percentage of the black vote reaches double digits, in this case 16%, you're bound to get somebody's attention. So while national trends show the GOP struggling for decades to reach 10% of the black vote, in 2004 the total number of black votes cast for the president in Ohio had increased by more than 100% over his numbers in 2000.

How did the GOP manage it? In general terms, I'd sum it up this way: Committed black Christians believe in the sanctity of human life and traditional marriage as much as committed white Christians, maybe even more so, and in Ohio they decided to vote their beliefs. This alignment of conscience with action alarmed the Reverends Jackson and Sharpton, who began to see their 'sheep' showing signs of independent reflection and thought. So Jackson and Sharpton decided to strike back and this is where they, in my opinion, crossed the line.

They began a campaign across the country to "refocus" the black churches on the real ills that plague black society: poverty and social injustice, to be exact. That's okay. Good people of all races are concerned about these issues.

They confronted these issues, however, by creating bogeymen, building walls and dividing people, which is a page straight out of the Democratic Party playbook, "How to Keep 'Em Mad and on Our Side," rather than building bridges and uniting them.

Here's what really got the hairs on the back of my neck standing up. They stated that issues like abortion and same-sex marriage weren't relevant to the black faith community and we should ignore them because they distract us from the real problem, presumably Republicans and their policies.

The reverends went on to say that most black people don't know someone in a same-sex marriage or who's had an abortion, but they know plenty of people who are poor or victimized by social injustice. Given that one of every two black pregnancies ends with an abortion, I am skeptical of the claim that most black people don't know someone who has aborted a baby.

I sat in the pews at a local black church the Sunday before the 2006 general election and heard the pastor, a friend and associate of the Rev. Jackson, faithfully deliver this "refocused" message to his congregation. He delivered this blatantly political, partisan sermon after introducing all the candidates who were visiting. He then promptly patted himself on the back for his non-partisan behavior.

While there were many contributing factors to the GOP's significant electoral defeats in 2006, I'm convinced this campaign on the part of these two famous reverends was effective in achieving their goal of herding the "flock" back into the barn.

I had only one response to these talking points masquerading as the inspired Word of God: "Say what?"

Did God rewrite the Bible and forget to tell us? Did He change His mind on the sanctity of human life, which He created in His image, or traditional marriage, which He created to raise, protect and nurture children?

Of course He didn't.

The economic justice reverends and their liberal friends love to point out how many more references there are in the Bible to caring for the poor and advocating justice than to abortion or homosexuality, so God must think those are much more important. That's such a human way of thinking and even well-meaning conservative Christians tend to enumerate God's words to emphasize a favored position on a particular issue.

Here is what I believe: If God said it, then He means it. Period. It doesn't matter how many times He said it. The very second He uttered the words, they came imbued with all the authority of the Creator and Redeemer. Therefore, only one response is truly justified: obedience.

As to their statements that the taking of unborn human life and the breakdown of traditional marriage aren't important to the black community, I have to ask them, "Are you mad?"

Seventy-two percent of black births are to women who can't or won't get married, and there's a straight line from the staggering numbers of births out of wedlock to the struggles of our young black men who didn't have the love or modeling of a devoted father in their homes. Because they don't know how to be men, they behave as boys—except they are bigger and carry more dangerous toys, so they leave much bigger messes behind for someone else to clean up, and they hurt people when they play rough.

Black women are over three times more likely to get an abortion than any other demographic in America. Since 1973, millions of black babies have been aborted at a cost to black people of $4 billion! What would these communities look like if that $4 billion had been invested in alternative schools, micro-loans to small businesses, or development of entrepreneurial skills?

Again, not only are 80% of Planned Parenthood's abortion facilities located in minority communities, their school-based clinics target black, minority and ethnic schools.

In Louisiana, Planned Parenthood proposed placing its school-based clinics *only in predominantly black schools*. When a black state legislator suggested that they place them in predominantly white schools too, the proposal was dropped.

Given that Planned Parenthood's founder, Margaret Sanger advocated population control of the "unfit," I'm convinced she would approve of their actions today. I also believe the same disregard for human life promoted in the black community by the abortion industry is what leads to 94% of blacks murdered in the U.S. being killed by other blacks.

In 1977, a black leader righteously declared, "Abortion is black genocide." He said:

> *That is why the Constitution called us three-fifths human and then whites further dehumanized us by calling us "niggers." It was part of the dehumanizing process. The first step was to distort the image of us as human beings in order to justify that which they wanted to do and not even feel like they had done anything wrong. Those advocates of taking life prior to birth do not call it killing or murder, they call it abortion. They further never talk about aborting a baby because that would imply something human. Rather they talk about aborting the fetus. Fetus sounds less than human and therefore abortion can be justified.[17]*

Those powerful words came from Rev. Jesse Jackson, the same black leader who now calls on the black church to ignore abortion as an issue.

While Jackson's fidelity to sacred scripture was questionable in other areas of sexual morality, he was once an eloquent and moral voice against procured abortion. He declared in an open letter to Congress that "as a matter of conscience I must oppose the use of federal funds for a policy of killing infants."[18]

Somewhere along the way, he and the majority of the black church decided that political power was more valuable than obeying the Lord Who knew us and called to us while we were still in the womb. The black church silenced itself to gain favor in political circles, yet every Sunday the congregations dance, sing and shout to God Who grieves as the blood of unborn innocents cries out to Him, drowning out their displays of emotion.

Politics isn't the only force that perverted the black church. The 1960s saw the rise of so-called black liberation theology, an outgrowth of the more radical elements of the civil rights movement.

Liberation theology had infected many Catholic parishes in Latin America. Even though the Catholic Church had long condemned Marxism, many preachers in Latin America twisted the Gospel to pit the oppressed against the perceived oppressors, and they called for a socioeconomic revolution rather than true salvation.

Both brands of liberation theology essentially wrap Marxist revolutionary dogma in the veneer of Christianity, disguising a failed political ideology and making it more appealing to the poor peasants of central and South America, and the poor blacks of North America.

Black liberation theology came to the general public's attention during the 2008 presidential campaign when one of its practitioners, the Rev. Jeremiah Wright, was exposed in a series of self-produced videotaped sermons preaching hatred. For example, there is his 'God Damn America' sermon. Wright also bolstered his case for racism against whites by claiming that Jesus was a "poor black man." Granted, Jesus the Israeli probably wasn't fair skinned, but He didn't have the complexion of an African either. Anyway, once Wright was exposed, he declared that black liberation theology is a legitimate expression of Christianity and it was simply misunderstood by whites.

Had Wright not been Barack Obama's "spiritual mentor," he may have faded into oblivion. Had Obama not claimed that he gave his life over to Christ in Wright's Chicago church, Wright would have remained a neighborhood idol. Yet Obama married Michelle there and said he had his daughters baptized there too.

So the very fact that the Obamas had listened to Wright and worshipped at his church for over 20 years was totally at odds with the post-partisan, post-racial image that the presidential candidate tried to project. Eventually, Obama had to publicly jettison his "spiritual mentor" to reclaim his aura of mass appeal.

While the controversy didn't impede Sen. Obama's ascent to the presidency, it exposed a version of Christianity that is foreign to most Americans but all too prevalent in the black community.

The father of black liberation theology, the Rev. James H. Cone, sums up this false teaching in his own words:

> *Black theology refuses to accept a God who is not identified totally with the goals of the black community. If God is not for us and against white people, then he is a murderer, and we had better kill him. The task of black theology is to kill gods who do not belong to the black community...*
>
> *Black theology will accept only the love of God which participates in the destruction of the white enemy. What we need is the divine love as expressed in Black Power, which is the power of black people to destroy their oppressors here and now by any means at their disposal. Unless God*

is participating in this holy activity, we must reject his love.[19]

The very notion that God segregates people by race, or that one race is inherently demonic and must be destroyed, is vile and spits in the face of Christ, Who came to "seek and to save that which was lost."[i] Remember, the creation account in Genesis specifies that each of us, male and female, is created in the image and likeness of God. So the Gospel of Christ is a message of salvation for all humankind, not earthly revenge, redistribution of wealth or coercive power for some over others.

The other false teaching that has taken hold in some black churches is commonly called the "prosperity gospel." Essentially, its preachers seek to persuade black people that the Gospel message is about becoming rich as a reward for faith. Usually, the only ones getting rich on the prosperity gospel are the very same preachers who demand money and gifts from their gullible followers.

Now let's put this into perspective. Jesus Christ equated serving the poor with serving Him. He was the rabbi Who chased the merchants out of the temple with a whip fashioned by His own hands. Clearly, He regards hawking riches in His name as vile. Clearly, He condemns black liberation theology or any other false teaching that distracts from the "good news of great joy which will be for all the people."[j]

The black church has become too immersed in the world and corrupted by power, influence, money or a combination of these earthly passions. In that regard, they are little different than many Christian churches

---

[i] Luke 19:10.

[j] Luke 2:10.

which have forgotten the words of their Lord, Who declared, "My Kingdom is not of this world."[k]

While the role of government is to protect the lives and rights of others, the teaching and promotion of public virtue is the realm of the church, and the Christian church, the predominant faith in America, has failed to be a transcendent, unshakeable force for public virtue.

The consequences of these worldly distractions, however, are magnified when it comes to the black church because of its preeminence in the black community, and the power it has to influence the actions of its congregants and the communities in which they live. To paraphrase an old saying, when the church in America sneezes, black churches catch a cold.

The black church's role as a sanctuary to the black community cannot be understated. From the beginning, it was the center of the neighborhood, a gathering place not only for worship and spiritual instruction, but also for fellowship and social activism. The civil rights movement was essentially a faith-based movement and the black church took the lead to help secure our rights and ensure equal justice.

Yet today, the black church looks away while 17 million black babies and counting are slaughtered by the abortion industry in America, solely because the black church wishes to appease the Democrats to whom they have promised fealty.

It is folly for the black church to fear the wrath of men more than the wrath of God. There will be an accounting one day, not just for the millions of babies murdered, but also for all the people led astray from obedience to God for political purposes.

Dr. Martin Luther King, Jr. described the early church in the Acts of the Apostles as "not merely a thermometer that recorded the ideas and principles of

---

[k] John 18:36.

popular opinion; it was a thermostat that transformed the mores of society."

My challenge to the black church is to stop being a thermometer and start being a thermostat. If the black church stood as one against abortion and for traditional marriage, the Democratic Party would either be forced to change or would tear itself apart in the struggle.

That prospect shouldn't bother the faithful because we're not called to uphold worldly institutions, but instead to obey the Lord. Jesus asks us, "For what does it profit a man to gain the whole world, and forfeit his soul?"[1]

The seeds of revolution are already being planted. There is a growing black pro-life movement in this country and pastors are at its helm.

Likewise, black pastors are often at the forefront of defending marriage from being redefined into whatever humans desire.

I hope that all black pastors and their churches across the nation will join them and turn up the heat. After all, that's what a thermostat does.

---

[1] Mark 8:36.

5

Some Splainin' to Do

*"Never explain yourself. Your friends don't
need it and your enemies won't believe it."*
~ Belgicia Howell

"Why are you a Republican?"
I'd heard this question before, mostly from my
mother, and my glib answer, "That's how you raised
me," was usually enough to deflect the conversation to
some other topic.

This time, however, it was posed to me by some
stranger who got my cell phone number from Facebook.
"I have to take down that number," I muttered to myself
as the caller, not waiting to hear my answer, rattled off
how he worked for many rich people and saw their greed
firsthand.

I felt like asking him, "Why do you assume these
greedy rich people were Republicans? Did you ask them
for their voter registration cards?" However, I held my
tongue since I couldn't get a word in edgewise without
interrupting him. Oh, was he on a roll.

The stereotype of the rich or greedy Republican is just
another example of people making decisions with their
hearts rather than their heads. And that old chestnut is
blown to pieces by the evidence.

For example, 60% of contributions from the top
25 Wall Street firms go to Democrats. Four of the top
six overall donors to Democrats are Wall Street firms,
and one of those firms gave to Democrats by a 3-to-1

margin. Even Wall Street companies outside the top 25 gave 58% more to Democrats than Republicans.

Of the 535 members of the U.S. Congress, 237 of them (44%) are millionaires, compared to 1% of the general population. Now here's where it gets even more interesting: 54% of those 237 millionaires are Democrats. Of the top 10 richest people in Congress, eight are Democrats, and 16 of the top 25 are Democrats. Then again, 22 of the 30 wealthiest congressional districts in the country are represented by Democrats.

In Maryland, businesses overwhelmingly give to the most anti-business politicians in America and I'm flummoxed by their eagerness to surrender their hard-earned cash to elected officials who consistently tax and regulate them practically out of existence. Apparently, they're hoping to gain access and persuade politicians not to be too hard on them. It's pretty pathetic because these business owners have the power to help elect people who are for free markets and free trade, but they can't see past the next earnings statement.

As for Republicans (or more accurately conservatives) being greedy, this lie has been refuted consistently in study after study. It is most notably debunked by Arthur C. Brooks, former Syracuse University professor and president of the American Enterprise Institute, in his book, *Who Really Cares: The Surprising Truth About Compassionate Conservatism.*

Even *New York Times* columnist Nicholas Kristof lectured his fellow liberals in a column written during the 2008 holiday season. In "Bleeding Heart Tightwads," Kristof said, "We liberals are personally stingy." He further professed to "shame liberals into being more charitable" and he challenged them to put "your wallets where your hearts are."

Of course, I never had a chance to explain any of this to my caller, who was clearly more intent on transmitting than receiving.

At one point, however, he started complaining about the lack of good jobs in the state and wondered why we couldn't attract businesses like our neighbors on the other side of the Potomac in northern Virginia. I thought, "Are you kidding? You can't demand jobs while hating the ones who create them!" Well, apparently he could.

After my caller hung up, I thought about his initial question and concluded it was the only part of the conversation that made any sense. Had he been someone honestly seeking an answer, I know how I would have responded. It's a question I first addressed publicly in 2001, the year after the contentious presidential campaign between Al Gore and George W. Bush. It's the question I addressed again after the election of our first black president, Barack Obama.

My family and I lived in Florida during the historic and infamous recount that followed the 2000 general election. I ached for my adopted home state because each side was declaring nefarious intent regarding the unfortunate yet easily explainable events.

Whether it was ballot design, poorly trained volunteer poll workers, voting sites overwhelmed by unanticipated voter turnout, or some other circumstance or set of circumstances, people were becoming agitated over occurrences that I am convinced took place in every state in the Union. Florida just happened to be the epicenter of the Electoral College that year, and was therefore subjected to intense scrutiny which no state could hope to escape unscathed.

I was particularly incensed by the charge that racism was behind the inability of voters in predominantly black neighborhoods in south Florida to cast their ballots. The race drew a high turnout in many minority precincts. That was unexpected and exceeded the trends of the recent past. Since the recruitment and training of volunteer poll workers was based on an underestimated turnout, problems were sure to crop up.

Yet this explanation was not sinister enough for the race merchants and conspiracy theorists. So they alleged an orchestrated effort to suppress black voter turnout.

I remember thinking how foolish we blacks must seem to more rational people when we make such wild accusations. If I recall correctly, I wrote a letter to my local paper ridiculing the whole notion of black voter suppression in the 21st century. After all, I was able to walk into my local voting place, which was well-staffed and its volunteer poll workers well-trained. I was able to cast my ballot without anyone attempting to block me or guide me toward voting a certain way. I concluded that since I was obviously black, the conspiracy was either run by incompetents or it was the product of fevered imagination or cynical manipulation.

Subsequent to the Supreme Court decision that led to George W. Bush being declared the winner of the 2000 general election and inaugurated as our 43rd president, I was watching his nominee for attorney general of the United States, former U.S. Senator John Ashcroft, being grilled by the race merchants on the Senate Judiciary Committee.

Central to their accusations of racism was his opposition while in the Senate to the appointment of a black Missouri Supreme Court judge to a lifetime federal judgeship. Clearly, they huffed, this was indicative of his vile racist heart. But in his book *Never Again,* Ashcroft calmly explains his reasoning:

> *Studying his judicial record, considering the implications of his decisions, and hearing the widespread objections to his appointment from a large body of my constituents, I simply came to the overwhelming conclusion that Judge White should not be given lifetime tenure as a U.S. District Court judge.*

Never Again is a great title which, although it referred to Ashcroft's resolve in the war on transnational terrorism, could have also described his disgust with the bizarre world of Washington, DC.

Ashcroft had judged this man according to the content of his character—imagine that! But that's not really what the race merchants want, despite their claims to the contrary.

I hated to see the character assassination of John Ashcroft. In the realm of politics, many knew him as a decent, honorable man devoted to God, his family and friends. Many knew his record of commitment to the laws of the nation and so they expected him to uphold the law with distinction. I have since had the honor of meeting him in person and spending some time with him, and I can confirm that he is every bit the humble and moral gentleman I believed he was.

The fact that he appointed the first black judge to the Western District Court of Appeals while governor of Missouri, and that he voted for the vast majority of minority nominees while a U.S. senator, further contributed to my frustration with the demagogues of race.

In response, I did what I typically do when an issue has me up in arms. I wrote down my thoughts and shared them with the public. If I ever run for national office, I'm going to give some opposition research team migraines because I've been writing for public consumption since I won my first award from the Freedoms Foundation at Valley Forge in 1976. I'm sure there's something in all those years of writing essays, letters and op-ed pieces that they'd try to use against me, but my writing also reflects the evolution and growth of a human being, so I have no qualms whatsoever about what they might find.

My thoughts on the race merchants and their manipulation of the facts to suit their worldview became an essay published in the Fall 2001 issue of what was then the Florida Republican Party's periodic magazine, *The*

Triumph, and it was entitled "Young, Republican and Black":

In the past, being African-American and a Republican made me nothing more than an oddity to my family members and a curiosity to others. Due to recent events, however, the hostility between African-Americans and the Republican Party is greater than I've ever seen it. Nine out of 10 African-Americans voted against President Bush in the recent election.

Well, I'm number 10—I've been a Republican since college, and I voted for George Bush. Since the mainstream press and civil rights advocacy groups tell only one side of the African-American story, let me share with you my reasons for being a Republican.

1. The GOP respects my values.

I'm not only a Republican, but also a devout Christian, dedicated to following Jesus Christ's example in all areas of my life, including my role as a citizen. The GOP's position on social issues, especially abortion, resonates with my religious beliefs. That is not to say that people who profess faith in Christ can't be Democrats; indeed, millions of Christians claim an affinity for the Democratic Party as the party of the working class and the oppressed. However, the Republican Party enthusiastically embraces born-again Christians, and respects the role Christ plays in our everyday lives. The Democratic Party, on the other hand, seems uncomfortable with us and treats us like that eccentric relative you try to hide from your friends. The party's implicit message to committed Christians is that faith in Christ is private and should be kept to oneself - after all, you might offend someone!

Besides, it may be all well and good for Sundays, but not every day of the week. The notion that I'm to keep my allegiance to Christ to myself, or relegate it to some compartment that is distinct from other areas of my life, is patently offensive. Being a Christian is a way of life - as authors Bruce Bickel and Stan Jantz put it, "If what you believe doesn't affect how you live, then it isn't very important." My political affiliation lies with the party that appreciates that fact and isn't embarrassed by my beliefs.

2. I'm suspicious of the herd mentality.

In my view, something's amiss when over 90% of a particular demographic group votes the same way because, generally, you won't find 90% of any group of people that thinks or acts the same. No one would be so presumptuous as to claim that all women (43% for Bush), or Asians (41% for Bush), or Hispanics (35% for Bush), or labor union members (40% for Bush), share the same beliefs. In fact, the voting patterns of most demographic groups reflect the diversity of beliefs and opinions that normally exist within a community. When one group of people votes overwhelmingly and consistently for the same party, I question whether they have arrived at their decisions independently, or if they are depending solely on what their self-proclaimed leaders tell them.

I personally know many blacks whose worldview is as conservative as my own, yet would rather follow the Rev. Jesse Jackson's lead than vote their beliefs. I don't need his mind to make my decisions for me; that's why God gave me a mind of my very own—and I'd rather not waste it.

3. Racial fear mongering does not move me.

The African-American community is decrying a racist "conspiracy," which prevented many blacks from voting in the recent election. The explanation that many predominantly black precincts, which historically have not had heavy voter turnouts, were overwhelmed and unprepared, or that many of the people who showed up at the polls were first-time voters and not experienced in how to cast their ballots, is not sinister enough for the conspiracy theorists.

There are certainly systemic problems that need to be addressed, but they weren't the product of an orchestrated effort to deny blacks the right to vote: Similarly, the accusation by civil rights groups that Attorney General John Ashcroft is racist doesn't hold up when his record of appointments in the state of Missouri, or his overwhelmingly favorable votes in the U.S. Senate to confirm black candidates for federal judgeships, is examined.

The sad fact is that the Democrats and mainstream civil rights groups have used these scare tactics to mobilize the African-American vote against Republicans for many years now. As a people often on the receiving end of race baiting throughout history, and who still are defamed by stereotypes designed to frighten whites, you'd think we'd know better.

I guess I'm looking for leaders who think more of me than to pander to my ethnicity. We are more than what appears to the naked eye, and racial politics are just as flawed when we engage in them as they are when used against us.

4. I believe in individual accountability and responsibility.

There is no shame in seeking help when we can't do something on our own. However, if we've reached that point, hopefully it is after we've exhausted all our resources and still met with failure. Our achievements in life should be the direct responsibility of the person we see in the mirror every morning, and we should be fully accountable, to our families, communities and our faith for doing the right thing to the best of our abilities—and to get back up again when we fall down.

When I consider the problems that plague the African-American community, very few of them have to do with laws or political action, and everything to do with individual choices. Neither the law nor political action have kept us from abusing illegal drugs, or having children out of wedlock, or murdering each other, nor have they kept us from running down our brothers and sisters who are striving because we portray the educated and academically inclined among us as less than black.

It breaks my heart to see us wasting energy on things other than building our people up to face the challenges and opportunities this internet-paced world places before them. We need to stand up loud and clear for strong moral values, academic excellence, abstinence from addictive substances or behaviors, and a "no excuses" perseverance that is always stronger than racism.

There are far too many accomplished African Americans in our country today for us to claim racism as the sole reason for our failings. If racism is that pervasive, then none of us would have "made it;" in fact, millions of us have. We need to instill individual self-esteem in our young people, rather than perpetuating the notion that everything bad that happens to us is the fault of an inherently racist society. I believe there are more people out there ready to help us than hurt us. At least, that has been my life experience, and it's been validated time and again.

In summary, you may not agree with my reasons for being a Republican, but they reflect who I am - a whole person. I am a Christian, father, husband, friend, neighbor, taxpayer, citizen, and yes, a black man. I can't ignore my African-American heritage, nor do I want to, because there is great strength in our history of persecution and overcoming.

It is only a part of who I am, however, and who I am inside is at least as important as who I am on the outside. We should encourage our richness and diversity *as a people rather than suffocate it under a blanket of conformity, which by its very nature loathes excellence.*

As I review what I wrote back in 2001, I don't think I'd change a word, except I wouldn't use the term "African-American." That was a concession to political correctness I won't make today. I have no more allegiance to Africa than most Americans of European descent have toward their countries of origin and I am truly blessed to be an American.

As it turns out, I wasn't done with public justifications of my party and ideological affiliation. The 2008 presidential campaign presented me with an opportunity, if you can call it that, to once again explain my views. The result was "Barack and Me," a September 13, 2009 essay published by the American Thinker website:

I've been a committed conservative and, with the exception of one year where I listed myself as an independent, a registered Republican since 1978. What makes that rather unremarkable statement more intriguing is that I'm an American who happens to be black.

Anyone who follows politics knows that puts me in rare and sometimes lonely company. Black voting percentages for the Republican nominee for President since 1964 are typically in the single digits, reaching 11% nationwide in 2004 and, perhaps more significantly, 16% in Ohio, helping George W. Bush take that state and the presidency for a second term. There is no single demographic group in the nation that is more loyal and, in my opinion, more taken for granted by the beneficiaries of their votes than blacks.

Until February 10, 2007, most of my black friends and associates tolerated my status as a conservative and Republican, dismissing me as a novelty or something less flattering but essentially harmless. After that date, and especially after the Iowa caucuses in the 2008 presidential election, I became an enemy and someone who needed to be silenced at all costs.

What changed? The emergence of Barack Hussein Obama as the first viable black candidate for the presidency, an occasion that called for racial solidarity over ideological purity or party loyalty.

I know I didn't change. I saw in Barack Obama not a black man but another liberal Democrat out to convince Americans to surrender their liberty for the benevolent dictatorship of government. To me, he was no different than Al Gore in 2000 or John Kerry in 2004.

That said, the first time I wrote about him was after reading his book, The Audacity of Hope, *and I was indeed hopeful that he might be different:*

> Yes, we are on opposite ends of the political spectrum, but his words suggest he seeks to understand and doesn't instantly dismiss people like me in the self-righteous and condescending way liberals have adopted when addressing their conservative counterparts.

I was further impressed with his efforts to transcend the racial politics of past Democratic presidential contenders, especially the man who preceded him as the most successful black candidate for president, the Rev. Jesse Jackson. In a subsequent article, I wrote:

> As a leader and manager in the military, the business world, government and the non-profit sector, I've learned that if we want people to follow us, we need to find a common goal toward which to strive, and we need to extend to them the presumption of good faith in the tone and tenor of our words and deeds. I think this is why Sen. Barack Obama's campaign for president of the United States is making history.

As the campaign wore on, however, I began to realize that he was as much a prisoner of the Democratic Party as so many other black politicians before him, and I didn't disguise my disappointment:

How, then, do I square my generally positive feelings about Barack Obama the man, and the significance of his run for the presidency to black Americans like me, with the fact that we agree on almost nothing when it comes to policy?

From that point forward, I was increasingly critical of Barack Obama and publicly declared my intention to vote for John McCain over him.

You would think I had donned a white robe and hood based on the reactions of my black friends. One even went so far as to say that Obama's blackness was reason enough for me and other blacks to vote for him. I shot back that when I ran against a long-time white incumbent for a state Senate seat in 2006, she and other blacks voted against me in droves so racial solidarity apparently only works one way.

I went on to evoke the old Zora Neale Hurston quote, "my skinfolk ain't necessarily my kinfolk," a phrase used often as a pejorative against blacks who don't toe the party line. In this case, I used it to shine the light on the naked hypocrisy of blacks who want unquestioned loyalty to Obama because he's black but call Republican National Committee chairman Michael Steele, the first black chairman of the GOP, a "house Negro."

Since his inauguration, the scope of President Obama's agenda and the speed with which he's attempting to implement it have brought out some of my most pointed criticism. I've come to realize his perception of America as an arrogant nation in need of forgiveness for its sins, his contempt for free enterprise, and his faith in government over individuals are irreconcilable differences, and we are destined to be permanently at odds barring some epiphany on his part or mine.

What usually follows my critiques is a chorus of angry questions and comments from other blacks who are quick to come to his defense and impugn my motives, intelligence, and even my ability to think independently. The latter point is ironic given that I'm not the one who's following the herd here, but I'm not writing this to defend myself.

Rather, I want to challenge these critics who seem to think I owe Barack Obama the benefit of the doubt because he's the first black President and I need to support him on that basis alone.

I believe with every fiber of my being that abortion is as great a moral stain on the consciousness of this nation as were slavery and institutionalized discrimination. The fact that, since 1973, it has killed more black people than all other causes of death in the black community combined is the cruelest of ironies.

Despite the fact most blacks agree with me, they are somehow able to overlook the legalized murder of voiceless, helpless children for convenience. I can't.

What do you expect me to say to a president who, regardless of color, is dedicated to removing all restrictions on abortion and considers it a right?

I believe that government is designed to defend our nation from foreign attack, provide for public safety, enforce the law and deliver equal justice for all. Beyond that, I do not want government to dictate to me how to raise my children, how much I can or can't earn, or the causes to which I can contribute.

I don't believe in enforced charity and I believe a government that does too much not only takes our freedom, but also our will to achieve and our desire to give, rendering us morally indolent.

Government says it will provide for us and we no longer have to provide for one another. This mindset has done great damage to the black community because government is a poor substitute for a father in the home, a neighbor with a helping hand, and the church down the street.

What do you expect me to say to a president who, regardless of color, believes in "spreading the wealth" and thinks people who work hard, play by the rules and are successful don't deserve to make more than what he thinks is "fair"?

I believe that America has done more to bring liberty and prosperity to the world than any other great nation in history, and all we ever asked for was the land to bury the more than 100,000 men and women who never made it home. I am a proud veteran who loves my country not because she is great but because she strives to be good.

What do you expect me to say to a president who travels the world apologizing not just for the perceived sins of the past eight years, but also for American wrongs that pale in comparison to the autocratic regimes to which he's apologizing?

I am a conservative. He is not.

I believe all human life is sacred and worthy of our protection. He does not.

I believe in individuals over government. He does not.

I believe America is a force for good in the world and has nothing for which to apologize. He does not.

What do you expect me to say?

In retrospect, I would have probably added the following statements to expound upon my beliefs:

I believe there is great wisdom in the lessons of history and I believe in prudence before making radical changes. Obama does not.

I believe there are truths which are eternal and not derived from man; therefore, they cannot be revoked, nor should they be ignored. He does not.

I believe the power of our nation is in its people exercising their liberties and not in government imposing its will on them. He does not.

President Obama is a typical Democrat. I cannot abide by the policies he and his fellow Democrats support.

And that, my cold-calling friend, is why I'm a Republican.

6

Coming Home

*"If ever influenced by the friendship of your Democratic
neighbor, you desert the Republican flag, desert the
Republican standard, desert the Republican Party that
freed you, you will be voting away your last liberties."
~ Hiram R. Revels, the first black American to serve
in Congress, elected in 1870 as a Republican*

Tavis Smiley had the Republican Party in his sights
and he wasn't going to pass up the opportunity to
take aim and fire.

The first of two live presidential forums sponsored
by the Public Broadcasting Service and moderated by
Mr. Smiley, a noted black author, journalist and commentator, took place on June 28, 2007 on the campus
of historically black Howard University in Washington,
DC. All eight of the Democratic candidates were there,
elbowing each other to see who could curry more favor
with voters of color.

Behind the scenes, Smiley and PBS had also spent
months in preparation for a similar forum for the
Republican candidates. And two prominent Republicans
encouraged them to host the event at another historically
black university, Morgan State University in Baltimore:
Maryland's former lieutenant governor, Michael Steele
(black), and former GOP chairman Ken Mehlman (white).

However, a funny thing happened on the way to the
forum and Mr. Smiley wasn't laughing. In fact, he was
fuming—in print, on TV and on the radio.

The men considered the four major Republican contenders at the time—former New York Mayor Rudy Giuliani, former Massachusetts Governor Mitt Romney, Sen. John McCain (AZ) and former Sen. Fred Thompson (TN)—had all declined to participate, citing scheduling conflicts. Some indicated that scheduling a forum in the last week of the fundraising cycle left them with a difficult choice between participation in the debate or raising desperately needed funds for their campaigns.

Mr. Smiley wasn't buying it and neither were the Republicans who worked with him to arrange this forum. Michael Steele insisted that the GOP frontrunners come to the table, saying "I think it's an important opportunity for Republican candidates to put up or shut up, when it comes to minority communities in the country." Former Secretary of Housing and Urban Development Jack Kemp, a Republican with a notable track record of outreach to minority voters since his days as a U.S. congressman from Buffalo, said, "[W]e sound like we don't want black people to vote for us. What are we going to do—meet in a country club in the suburbs one day? If we're going to be competitive with people of color, we've got to ask them for their vote."

Newt Gingrich, in my opinion the greatest thinker and intellectual force in the conservative arena today, was direct and unflinching in his criticism:

For Republicans to consistently refuse to engage in front of an African American or Latino audience is an enormous error. I hope they will reverse their decision and change their schedules. I see no excuse—this thing has been planned for months, these candidates have known about it for months. It's just fundamentally wrong. Any of them who give you that scheduling-conflict answer are disingenuous. That's baloney.

Finally, Smiley himself said to the *Washington Post*, "When you reject every black invitation and every brown invitation you receive, is that a scheduling issue or is it a pattern? I don't believe anybody should be elected president of the United States if they think along the way they can ignore people of color. That's just not the America we live in."

I was also annoyed, but not just at the four candidates who declined to participate. I was annoyed at the pundits and commentators for casting aspersions on the entire GOP because of those who didn't attend the forum rather than pointing out and praising the five candidates who did: former Arkansas Governor Mike Huckabee, Sen. Sam Brownback (KS), and Representatives Duncan Hunter (CA), Ron Paul, M.D. (TX) and Tom Tancredo (CO).

Practically all news references were highly critical of the GOP in its entirety and it seems most dismissed the participation of the lesser-known candidates. If we as people of color are sincere in our desire to have more choices in the political process, we need to resist the urge to smack down all Republicans regardless of their efforts and build up the ones who are trying to build bridges to us and our communities. Given that one of those lesser-known candidates, Mike Huckabee, eventually surged to the top tier in the months following the forum, and is now considered a major contender for the GOP presidential nominee in 2012, we dismiss the Republicans who seek a dialogue with us at our own peril.

I also think it's instructive to look at this through the lens of the absentee Republicans themselves. As a card-carrying Republican, I feel somewhat qualified to put words to how Republicans feel about reaching out to the mainstream black community.

Frankly, the belief among most Republicans is that black leaders and much of the black community immediately launch into insults and vitriol with the mere mention of the word "Republican" and they never get past that emotional reaction to actually have a constructive dialogue. They witness the verbal pounding taken by blacks who have the audacity to present themselves to the electorate as Republicans, and the sheer hypocrisy of white liberals using racist language and imagery to excoriate black conservatives while black liberals either let it happen or encourage it, and their reaction is "Thanks, but no thanks."

Let's be honest with ourselves: Politicians are not inclined to go where they believe they're unwelcome. When was the last time you saw a leading Democrat in front of a convention of pro-life, pro-traditional marriage advocates?

When I was running for office, I was routinely advised not to fill out a particular survey or attend a specific event because it was a no-win situation. The idea was that I couldn't win them over to my point of view and I'd probably say or write something that would end up in the papers and do more harm than good to my campaign.

The theory was that I had very little time to win people to my side, so it would've been a poor use of time and resources to court people who were hostile toward me before I even opened my mouth—hostile toward me simply for the "R" label.

There's another reason why Republicans are reluctant to appear before black audiences. When the Democrats failed to show up at the Family Research Council's Values Voters Summit held about the same time as the aforementioned GOP candidates' forum, there may have been an outcry similar to that over the PBS-sponsored forum in Baltimore, but I'll bet no one heard about it—I certainly didn't.

Republicans believe it's because their message is marginalized within the mainstream media, while liberal blacks have a louder megaphone and are given ample opportunity to use it when they are aggrieved. Republicans think that if they screw up in front of a black audience, they will hear about it in 7.1 channel surround sound and it will be played over and over again on the evening news and in the front pages of the major newspapers. Again, ask a campaign strategist whether or not he wants to take that risk and he'll glance at you sideways with a patronizing look before he walks away to consider more sensible options.

So the bottom line is that Republicans are afraid that blacks hate them just because they're Republicans and they won't be able to say anything without being publically pilloried on all major news outlets. To those who wish to see a greater dialogue between the black community and the Republican Party, and I count myself in that number, we need to figure out how to change the culture between these two groups. In my opinion, both sides have some growing up to do.

Republicans need to get a backbone and stand before all the people they hope to serve. Blacks need to get over their emotional attachment to one political party and become free agents in the political process if they don't want to be taken for granted.

Politics isn't "family," as one black constituent declared to a black Prince George's County Council member who dared to buck the black orthodoxy and endorse a black Republican in 2006 for the U.S. Senate in Maryland. Politics is business. It's a give and take between people who want something from each other and it takes dialogue to reach a consensus that works for both sides. If you refuse to talk, then reconciliation isn't possible.

I use the word "reconciliation" quite deliberately. Those who think the Democrats have always been the party of favor in the black community and the Republicans always on the margins haven't examined the history of racial politics in America.

Blacks probably know that Abraham Lincoln, the first Republican president, freed the slaves. He wasn't alone and he wasn't exactly a champion for equal rights for blacks, either, but let's go with that.

Until the early 1960s, the GOP was considered the party of civil rights. Yes, every major amendment to the Bill of Rights addressing equal protection under the law and equal citizenship was sponsored and passed by Republicans.

Every major piece of civil rights legislation, including the Civil Rights Act of 1957, was enacted by Republicans.

It was a Republican president, Dwight D. Eisenhower, who enforced the integration court order at Central High School in Little Rock, Arkansas by calling out the National Guard to escort the "Little Rock Nine" to classes that fateful September day in 1957.

Even the 1964 Civil Rights Act would have been defeated if Senate Minority Leader Everett Dirksen (R-IL) hadn't rallied the Republican Senate caucus on President Lyndon Johnson's behalf to thwart Democrats opposed to the measure. One of its chief opponents, Robert Byrd (D-WV),[m] continued to serve in the U.S. Senate until his death on June 28, 2010.

Republicans were also instrumental in the passage of the Voting Rights Act of 1965.

Richard Nixon, considered by many as the least likable Republican in history, got 32% of the black vote in the 1960 presidential race. But the next Republican nominee for president in 1964? Just 4%. No Republican presidential candidate has gotten more than 15% since then.

So what happened?

---

[m] Byrd was an admitted "former" member of the Ku Klux Klan.

The GOP began to lose its grip on the black vote under President Herbert Hoover; a pro-business Republican who many say failed to engage government to rescue those suffering from the Great Depression. President Franklin Roosevelt oversaw a massive expansion of government to lift the nation out of the Depression and, while scholars and political analysts continue to debate over the long-term consequences of his "New Deal," it's clear that the black community, which suffers the most during national economic downturns, benefitted greatly from it.

Another factor was the Republican Party's philosophical embrace of federalism, the division of roles and responsibilities between the federal and state governments to prevent the abuse of power by a centralized government. The Tenth Amendment states, "The powers not delegated to the United States by the Constitution, nor prohibited by it to the States, are reserved to the States respectively, or to the people."

While the amendment was written to protect the people from an overly intrusive and paternalistic central government, it was abused in practice by states, particularly in the South, which declared "states' rights" and condemned federal intervention in their affairs in order to defend legalized segregation.

The term "states' rights" comprised the official name of the "Dixiecrats," who broke away from the national Democratic Party in 1948 and created the States' Rights Democratic Party to defend the Southern "way of life" which included depriving blacks of their civil liberties under the Constitution.

Throughout most of the GOP's history, it emphasized liberty and equal justice and it used the power of the federal government to ensure the rights of all people were protected. When Republicans underwent a philosophical shift in the early 1960s and began to preach the supremacy of state governments over the federal government, blacks left the GOP in droves because they perceived "states' rights" as anathema to their interests.

Sen. Barry Goldwater (R-AZ), the leader of the new conservative movement within the GOP and an ardent proponent of states' rights, made a statement in Atlanta in 1961 that eventually turned the Rev. Dr. Martin Luther King, Jr., the most prominent black leader of his time, against him and the Republican Party:

> *We're not going to get the Negro vote as a bloc in 1964 and 1968, so we ought to go hunting where the ducks are.*

Despite the fact that, up to that point in his tenure as a U.S. senator, Goldwater had supported every major civil rights bill that came before him, the black community was critical of his comments. In their opinion, he was effectively saying "GOP to Blacks: Drop Dead." When Sen. Goldwater subsequently voted against the Civil Rights Act of 1964, ostensibly because he considered it federal intrusion into state matters, and became the Republican nominee for President in 1964, Dr. King was compelled to speak out. In *The Autobiography of Martin Luther King, Jr.*, he wrote:

> *While not himself a racist, Mr. Goldwater articulated a philosophy which gave aid and comfort to the racist. His candidacy and philosophy would serve as an umbrella under which extremists of all stripes would stand. In the light of these facts and because of my love for America, I had no alternative but to urge every Negro and white person of goodwill to vote against Mr. Goldwater and to withdraw support from any Republican candidate that did not publicly disassociate himself from Senator Goldwater and his philosophy.*

While I had followed a policy of not endorsing political candidates, I felt that the prospect of Senator Goldwater being President of the United States so threatened the health, morality, and survival of our nation, that I could not in good conscience fail to take a stand against what he represented.

Sen. Goldwater's philosophy did not win him the election but it planted the seeds of a Republican political strategy which sought to attract disaffected white Southerners to the party. This was the birth of the "Southern strategy" that Richard Nixon's political advisors employed to break "the solid South" and move voters into the GOP column. Nixon picked up five southern states during the 1968 presidential race, despite the independent candidacy of an avowed segregationist, Alabama Governor George Wallace.

In 1972, Nixon swept the South, an unprecedented feat for a Republican candidate of recent vintage.

In 1980, presidential candidate Ronald Reagan gave a speech near Philadelphia, Mississippi. That is the scene of the June 21, 1964 murder of three civil rights workers. Reagan declared, "I believe in states' rights." The use of what many people considered a code phrase for legalized segregation and the location he chose to give his speech led many to accuse him of appealing to the latent racism of white Southerners. The separation between blacks and the GOP was complete and apparently irreversible.

There are some Republicans who are critical of any minority outreach that first requires an apology for the "Southern strategy." They say the strategy was not racist but sought to reach out to all Southerners who felt abandoned as the Democratic Party began embracing positions that disrespected their religious values, economic interests and their support for national security and public safety. Others believe that apologizing to a group of people who will never respect the gesture is humiliating and meaningless. I have two responses to this line of reasoning.

First, if you think race wasn't at least a key factor in the "Southern strategy," then you're not paying attention. Even if one accepts the argument that these contenders for the presidency were ignorant of the emotionally charged nature of their words and actions, their advisors certainly weren't. When the GOP nominee kicks off his general election campaign in a location infamous in civil rights history and uses the term "states' rights" to describe his beliefs, it's virtually impossible to conclude that race had nothing to do with it.

Second, a sincere apology is a great starting point for a constructive dialogue that will benefit the GOP and the black community. Those who adopt the principle of politics as war may never accept this idea, viewing an apology as tantamount to surrender. Yet I believe it's time for both sides to acknowledge that they need each other and someone has to make the first move.

The GOP needs the black community if it's to become a true mainstream party. There is plenty of diversity in the black community and moderate to conservative blacks will give the Republicans a serious look if they pay more than lip service to black issues and concerns.

Blacks need the GOP so they can expand their options on the political menu and keep both major parties attuned to their agenda. Their overwhelming allegiance to the Democrats means they can be taken for granted by one party and ignored by the other. Whatever one may think of the GOP, the DNC's agenda is anything but an advantageous political arrangement for the black community in the 21st century.

So, can blacks and the GOP reconcile? I think it can happen, but a generational change will have to occur first. The hard feelings between the blacks of the civil rights era and the Republican Party run too deep. Even so, I believe that some concrete steps can and should be taken today to reconcile these two warring factions.

Discard all "50% Plus One" electoral strategies – Today's politics are based less on building a consensus among as many people as possible and more on maximizing the support of those who agree with you and discarding the rest. We need to stop that. As a former candidate for public office, I understand that a campaign has limited time and resources to deliver its message. I know campaigns must concentrate on communities where they can generate the greatest return. Today the margin of error is so slim that I don't believe either party can afford to ignore anyone. Electoral strategies that seek to polarize are not only unlikely to work in the end; they are inconsistent with American values.

Go if you're invited – If you're a Republican and the NAACP invites you to speak to them, go. Don't miss an opportunity to speak to audiences that don't traditionally embrace you. Look at it as a teaching and learning opportunity for both sides.

Find common ground – Blacks and GOP social conservatives share a deep religious conviction and hold the same views on many issues which have their origins in the faith community. Surveys suggest common ground on offering parents more choices for educating their children and protecting private property rights. The rising class of black entrepreneurs is open to economic policies that expand opportunities for minority business ownership and the creation of generational wealth that can be passed on to their children.
Developing a GOP agenda for the black community doesn't require a compromise of Republican values, just a broadening of the mind to view issues from another's perspective. Those who object to an agenda which caters

to a particular segment of society are either naïve or worse. Politics are all about building coalitions to achieve victory and that means communicating in the language and approach of those whose support you seek.

Pick your battles – There are issues which have great significance and meaning in the black community, but have been rejected by Republicans on philosophical grounds or for political expediency. Each rejection adds another brick to the wall dividing the GOP and the black community.

For example, the District of Columbia's pursuit of a voting representative to the U.S. Congress has consistently been blocked time and again by Republicans who hold up the Constitution in defense of their position, but it just reinforces their brand identity as racists in the eyes of the more than 580,000 people, mostly black, who want the same voice in the U.S. Congress as their fellow Americans.

I don't believe that our Founding Fathers intended for hundreds of thousands of American citizens to be regulated and taxed without representation in their federal government. It was a Republican, Rep. Tom Davis of Virginia, who championed legislation to grant the District's residents a voting representative in Congress. Two prominent black Republicans, RNC Chairman Michael Steele, as well as former Congressman J.C. Watts of Oklahoma, called on Republicans to pass the legislation.

The Republican Party should honor its historical heritage and free the citizens of the District from "taxation without representation." Amend the Constitution if that is what it takes.

This is just one example of how a change in position could earn the GOP some goodwill in the black community. Another would be correcting inequities in the criminal justice system that punish poor black drug addicts more than rich white ones. Republican presidential candidate Mike Huckabee embraced this position. He also supported rehabilitation and reentry into society for non-violent drug offenders while governor of Arkansas. He believes in sentencing reforms based on equal justice rather than revenge, a policy which, in the eyes of the black community, would correct what they perceive as an inherent bias against blacks in the system. The bottom line is that Republicans need to remember that a hand extended in friendship is better received when there's a gift in it.

Embrace your heritage – Some people see no relationship between the Republican Party created in 1854 and the GOP of today. I disagree. The one characteristic that is consistent throughout the party's history is its emphasis on individual liberty, whether it's liberty from the chains of slavery, liberty from oppressive Jim Crow laws, or liberty from a paternalistic government that stifles individual initiative and industry.

In that context, I see no incongruity with the black community's ongoing quest for equal justice. There is no liberty without justice and the administration of justice to uphold our nation's most cherished ideals is a fundamental function of government. When institutions within our borders fail to honor individual liberty, the GOP ought to be at the forefront of enforcing liberty as an unalienable right not only of Americans but all of humankind.

Thicken your skin – Initially, Republicans can do all of these things and demonstrate a genuine commitment to reconciliation with the black community, yet we'll still be heckled and insulted, we'll still be the targets of racially charged language not normally allowed in civil discourse and we won't get any credit for the things we do in support of the black community. That's just the way it is. We're not going to change the tone and tenor of this fractured relationship overnight.

I am optimistic about the opportunity for reconciliation because I've witnessed more people on both sides willing to ask questions and examine issues based on their merits rather than react with their emotions. The GOP is reassessing itself after the electoral defeats of 2006 and 2008, and this presents a golden opportunity for us to rethink assumptions and policies that have guided our party for over 40 years. The black community is beginning to suspect that their unfettered allegiance to one party isn't in their long-term best interests and is waiting for the Republicans to give them a proposal to consider.

My optimism notwithstanding, it's still not going to be easy or fun, especially if you're a black Republican. You have to decide right up front that it is important enough to the wellbeing of blacks and the GOP to bring these two historical allies together again. Once you've made that decision, you must gird yourself for battle and fight the good fight until you're no longer able to do so. You may not see the fruits of your labors, but your children will. It is my hope and prayer that our children will see a nation where ideas, rather than race, determine one's politics.

Reaching that point in our relationship with the GOP is critical to our survival, in my opinion, because the ideas which have held the black community hostage for the past 50 years are destroying us.

7

Defending Scoundrels

"He may be a son of a bitch,
but he's our son of a bitch."
~ attributed to FDR

The "trial of the century" was about to end and I remember stopping whatever I was doing to watch the verdict on television. The trial of former football star O.J. Simpson, accused of murdering his ex-wife, Nicole Brown, and her acquaintance Ronald Goldman, had all the elements of a bad pulp fiction novel. It had torn off the scab covering the nation's racial wounds, thanks to Johnny Cochran's skillful manipulation of the trial from a murder case to a referendum on racism in the police force. I was glad to see it was nearly over and awaited the guilty verdict I knew was sure to come.

When the words "not guilty" emanated from the television speakers, I was stunned, as were many of the people in the room with me. What I saw next on the TV screen blew my mind. A split screen showing a predominantly white audience on one side and a mostly black audience on the other, revealed starkly different reactions to the verdict. While the mostly white audience was stunned into silence, the mostly black audience erupted into wild cheers and celebration. It's almost as if we'd been watching different trials.

In the weeks to come, a furious debate ensued over the role of race in the verdict. Whites believed justice had been denied because a predominantly black jury reacted on emotion rather than the evidence.

Blacks believed justice had finally been served after decades of verdicts which either wrongfully convicted black men of crimes they didn't commit or set free white men who had maimed, killed or otherwise harmed black people.

They pointed out that the standard of reasonable doubt had been met by the defense and, therefore, acquittal was the right outcome, regardless of whether or not he actually committed the crime. They applauded the outcome as a small positive step of many that would be needed to balance out the injustices of the past.

In effect, O.J. Simpson grew to represent more than a jealous ex-husband accused of murdering his former spouse and her presumed boyfriend. He *became* black America and through him all blacks were on trial, and all were acquitted.

They also believed that Simpson's situation offered a valuable lesson to black men on how tenuous their status can be in the white community.

As a successful athlete and entertainer, O.J. Simpson had, in the eyes of many whites, transcended race. In fact, most blacks felt he had abandoned them.

He never spoke out on civil rights issues like one of his NFL predecessors, Jim Brown. He spent more time on the golf course at the local country club than in the dilapidated gyms of the inner city. He divorced his black wife and eventually married a blonde, voluptuous white woman, yet another "trophy" representing his success. He didn't confront or challenge anyone and he gave whites the cover they sought to profess their color-blindness and liberation from racism.

Once he was accused of murder, however, he was "just another nigger" in the eyes of whites—or so the black community would have you believe. The fact that the murdered woman was a blonde beauty added the tensions of interracial sex to the mix.

Blacks were frustrated with the attention Nicole Brown's murder received when black women who died at the hands of their husbands or boyfriends barely merited a mention in the crime section of the local papers. They saw this inattention as yet another diminution of black women by white society, comparable to the sexual exploitation of slave women by their white masters.

According to some observers, whites saw in Nicole Brown's brutal murder a vindication of their warnings to white women of the bestial nature of black men, a demeaning stereotype dating back to the days of slavery and meant to "protect" white womanhood.

Simpson himself recognized he had been abandoned by the society that had previously embraced him and he donned the full armor of racial persecution to win sympathy in the black community he had shunned. Blacks "took him back" in his hour of need and, as I indicated previously, his trial became their trial.

All of these race-related variables, and perhaps many more of which I'm unaware, played a prominent role in the disparate reactions of blacks and whites to the verdict. His subsequent civil trial, and the ruling which held him liable for the murders, kept racial tensions high. Some whites declared that a modicum of justice had been achieved and some blacks accused whites of vindictiveness because they didn't get their way in the criminal trial.

And me? I wasn't carrying all that baggage and much of what I learned about the various reactions to the verdict came well after the fact when people were being more candid and reflective about what had happened on that day.

At the time, I thought Simpson was guilty. He had a history of domestic violence, he was known to be jealous of Nicole Brown's lovers even though they were divorced and he'd all but confessed his guilt by leading the police on that infamous low-speed chase in his Ford Bronco.

I also thought his defense team, especially Johnny Cochran, did a masterful job of introducing reasonable doubt into the minds of the jurors. The prosecutors, perhaps overconfident because they presumed their case was open-and-shut, made mistakes that Cochran was quick to exploit. By the legal standards we set for capital murder cases, the verdict was the right one, so the question of whether or not he actually did it is irrelevant.

If you ask most people today, black or white, they'll tell you that they think O.J. Simpson is guilty of the murders. His recent arrest, trial and conviction for kidnapping and robbery, involving sports memorabilia he claimed was stolen from him, barely registered with the American public. Some think his 33-year sentence is justice delayed for the murders and most don't give him much thought at all.

That doesn't mean that we've grown up regarding the issues of race and justice. Another more recent and equally high-profile case also involved a star athlete, NFL quarterback Michael Vick, and the furor over his crimes once again exposed the racial divide in this country.

What brought this case home to me was a town hall meeting on the "Vick Divide" in Atlanta sponsored by ESPN. The "divide" referenced was between blacks and whites and their differing views on the Vick case. I was listening to the proceedings on the radio during my commute home and the meeting was so contentious that even the Atlanta director of the American Humane Society was shouted down by the mostly black audience for pointing out the horrific acts Vick had committed against defenseless animals.

As I listened, I found myself in a state of despair, wondering if we'd learned anything at all from the past. Here was a situation where the highest paid athlete in the NFL, heavily marketed as the face of the NFL and making silly amounts of money from huge endorsement deals, engaged in clearly illegal and unspeakably cruel activity for six years. His illegal activities were discovered by chance, not by design, and the preponderance of the evidence and the collusion of his accomplices with the authorities led him to plead guilty to federal crimes.

Right up to that time, he had lied to his teammates, the owner of the team, the NFL commissioner and the legion of fans who had bought his jersey and worn his shoes. He accepted full responsibility for his actions and blamed no one, not even his posse.

Yet when ESPN hosts a town hall meeting on the topic, it degenerates into a shout-down by a horde of black pro-Vick audience members who framed the issue in racial terms. They were rude to the panel members who held an alternative view, regardless of their race, and they even dismissed Vick's actions—federal offenses— as insignificant because the victims were "just dogs."

The Vick fans demonstrated an appalling lack of perspective by trying to compare his illegal and vicious behavior with that of New England Patriots head coach Bill Belichick, who had recently been punished by the NFL for filming the opposing team's defensive signals during a game.

Chuck Smith, a former teammate of Vick's and a black man, tried to point out the silliness of this analogy and he was booed lustily by the crowd. My heart sank.

I'll be honest—I was embarrassed by their behavior. One of the more irritating comments made during this town hall meeting was by another former teammate of Vick's, who is still very close to him. He admonished the listeners to be careful how they judge others because they'll be judged equally in return. The crowd erupted in cheers and it turned my stomach.

A month prior, another black athlete in trouble with the law, Travis Henry, declared that "only God can judge me" over his failure to pay child support for nine of the 11 children he procreated with 10 different women in four different states. I can't use the word "fathered" because he's no father.

The man made tens of millions of dollars as a running back in the NFL, but couldn't—or wouldn't—support his children. He then had the nerve to wrap himself in the Word of God to justify behavior that the Lord condemns without reservation or condition!

Incidentally, Henry was eventually released by his last team, the Denver Broncos. He also was arrested for and pled guilty to possession of cocaine with intent to distribute, and is currently serving 10 years to life in prison.

As a Christian, I know that God, the Creator and ultimate Judge, doesn't excuse my sins simply because I'm black. He forgives me, but only if I'm truly contrite, repentant and I change my ways.

Moreover, even the Lord's forgiveness doesn't excuse me from being held accountable for my actions. God clearly grants government the authority to enforce accountability for illegal actions and administer justice. Those who reject terrestrial judgment ought to read the 13th chapter of St. Paul's Letter to the Romans for God's view on the topic.

The only time we are to stand against the authorities of this earth is when their laws are in violation of God's laws, and we are to do so peacefully and respectfully. Dr. Martin Luther King, Jr. demonstrated in word and deed the Biblical way to stand against injustice. If he expended his precious moral capital on known scoundrels, I have neither read nor heard of it.

People who are either in trouble or defending others in trouble, and who hide behind God's grace by defiantly declaring "only God can judge me" ought to be careful what they wish for. As St. Paul says, "Do not be deceived, God is not mocked; for whatever a man sows, this he will also reap."[n]

We have a recent history of defending our scoundrels and rationalizing their actions because of the injustices committed against our ancestors. However, the weights and measures of equal justice are right and wrong, not black and white. If we are to be credible partners in calibrating the scales of justice so they work equally for everyone, we need to stand for right and wrong above all else.

The past is just that—the past. There is no way to reverse it or compensate for it. That is why the only true path to justice now and in the future is repentance, forgiveness and reconciliation. These actions should be familiar to all Christians and this approach is not only Biblical, but immensely practical given human nature. The long and tortured history shared by white and black Americans cannot be redone, but it can be redeemed through grace.

---

[n] Galatians 6:7.

Innocent Bystander

*"Experience is not what happens
to a man; it is what a man does
with what happens to him."*
~ Aldous Huxley

It seems like a long time ago, but Barack Obama wasn't always adored by the vast majority of the black community. In fact, when he announced his plan to run for president, not only was the black community skeptical of his chances, they were comfortably ensconced in Hillary Rodham Clinton's camp. Some 60% of likely black voters supported the former first lady over the freshman U.S. senator from Illinois.

At that time, one of the more prevalent questions about Barack Obama in the black community was whether or not he was "black enough." His upbringing gave no indication that he could relate to the history or the legacy of race relations in America. His mother was a white woman from Kansas, his father a black Kenyan. Neither came from a history of slavery or institutionalized discrimination. Instead, his mother's ancestors owned slaves and his father's ancestors had never stepped on American soil.

President Obama's formative years were spent in Hawaii and Indonesia, so his family was insulated from the turmoil of the American civil rights movement. When he wasn't with his mother, her parents raised him. Once on his own, Obama attended private colleges which were among the most elite institutions of higher learning in the nation. Because of his unique background and his exclusive education, many black observers and commentators perceived him as having lived a life that limited his exposure to the larger American black community and its struggles.

He wasn't helped by the image he projects either: cool, almost detached, intellectual, and academic in demeanor and presentation. His diction has very little of the inflections and cadences typically associated with black speech patterns. This, as we heard, resulted in more than one white politician referring to him as "articulate," which I didn't know was an insult to blacks until it was used to describe Sen. Obama.

While our political ideologies are polar opposites, on this point I identified to some extent with Sen. Obama. My life experiences left me with little or no exposure to the black struggle in America and that influenced my worldview.

While my parents are both black and were both born and raised in America, because of our travels as a military family, and where we lived most of the time, I wasn't exposed to the civil rights movement during my formative years.

By the time I was born in 1959, the U.S. armed forces had been integrated for just over a decade. That time period roughly coincides with the early years of the newest military service, the U.S. Air Force, which was established in 1947. My dad enlisted in the Air Force in 1957.

Although I was born in Louisiana, the state was more of a way station for us, a place where we'd camp out between my dad's duty assignments. Because of our nomadic lifestyle, I didn't spend a lot of time in the South during the 1960s. When Dr. King led the March on Washington in 1963, I was a four-year-old toddler in Alaska. When "Bloody Sunday" occurred in Selma,

Alabama, I was a kindergartner in Kokomo, Indiana. When the Black Power movement started to take hold in 1966 and riots broke out across the country in 1966 and 1967, I was an elementary school student in Japan.

I had no sense of black consciousness growing up because the world in which I lived didn't really call attention to my blackness as an issue or a cause. The civil rights movement wasn't a topic of discussion where I went to school and I don't recall talking about it at home with my parents. I went to integrated schools, lived in integrated housing, had many white friends and witnessed my parents entertaining blacks and whites in our home, all of them apparently enjoying each other's company. The only times I recall being more aware of race was when we were in Louisiana, since just about all the people I knew there were black, whether they were family or friends.

All of that changed for me in 1968 when my mother, my siblings and I stayed in Louisiana for a time while my father was finishing up his tour of duty in Japan and preparing for our next assignment to Idaho. I spent the latter half of third grade and most of fourth grade in Lake Charles and my life there was nothing like the Rockwellian experience of my previous years. Every face I saw at school—students, teachers and administrators—was black or brown.

Blacks lived on the north side of town and whites on the south side. The only time their worlds intersected was at work or when there was business to be transacted. The occasional white face would pop into our home if a friend of the family from one of our previous duty stations was passing through, but that was the extent of our social interaction with whites during that time.

Even then, I don't recall being conscious of why things were that way. I was idealistic and naïve, and didn't sense that anything was amiss other than we were in a different place. I simply expected everything would go back to normal when we transferred to my father's next assignment.

My awakening to the civil rights movement came right at the time it changed forever. I was in my grandparents' home the evening of April 4, 1968 when a special news bulletin flashed on the television screen and the reporter announced that Dr. Martin Luther King, Jr. had been assassinated in Memphis, Tennessee. I remember my grandparents and my mother reacting with great emotion and I knew that something terrible had happened, but I didn't understand the magnitude of it.

I was eight years old and, to my recollection, this was the first time I remember hearing his name. In the days to come, I became fully aware of Dr. King's legacy and martyrdom. My teacher had us all do a scrapbook of newspaper articles on the life of Dr. King. On the day of his funeral, regular instruction was suspended and televisions were wheeled into the classrooms so we could watch the proceedings.

I didn't think about it at the time, but I now presume the white children on the south side of town were having a normal school day with no acknowledgement whatsoever of Dr. King's life and death. In the days and weeks that followed, I did what I usually did when I wanted to learn more about something. I went to the library and checked out as many books as I could about Dr. King and the civil rights movement.

My thirst for knowledge turned to fear when Sen. Robert F. Kennedy was assassinated in Los Angeles in June of that same year. I remember going to bed that night thinking the world was coming to an end and that all good people were going to die. Even though school was out for the summer, I remember dutifully building a scrapbook on Sen. Kennedy and following his funeral on television. Blacks mourned his death almost as passionately as they did the death of Dr. King.

The names of Kennedy and King were revered by the black community, and it wasn't unusual in black households to see pictures of Sen. Kennedy's slain brother, President John F. Kennedy, and Dr. King on the mantle right next to a picture of Jesus Christ. Their sufferings raised them almost to the level of sainthood.

I remember the poignant song "Abraham, Martin and John" that came out soon after Sen. Kennedy's assassination, honoring Presidents Lincoln and Kennedy, and Sen. Kennedy and Dr. King for making the ultimate sacrifice for a greater good. The events of 1968 were a beginning for me, not only of my awareness of the black struggle for equality in America, but also of a passion for politics as a vehicle for social change.

Once my father returned from Japan and we moved on to our next duty station, life returned to "normal," or at least as I defined normal at the time. We moved to Mountain Home, Idaho and I'm sure the only black faces for miles were the military men and women and their families on the base.

Living once again in an integrated neighborhood and going to integrated schools, I practically forgot about the experiences of the previous year. I was still a political animal but had also become enraptured by Billy Graham and his crusades for Christ. I was probably one of the few boys who would run into the house from the playground to watch a preacher on TV! I also went door to door with my Bible in hand to "preach" to the neighbors. The adults thought I was cute but my peers hated me.

I continued my childhood of relative isolation from racial disharmony all the way through elementary school. Oh, there were a few incidents here and there. I recall some boy yelling "Nigger!" at me from across the road on the way to school one day, but I didn't respond and went about my business.

When my father was sent overseas to Thailand in 1971 for a one-year unaccompanied tour, the family returned to Lake Charles and there I endured the worst school year of my life. I was going into 7th grade at Lincoln Junior High School which, despite integration, was predominantly black. I soon found myself to be a fish out of water. The children there ridiculed my speech, accusing me of "talkin' propah" or "talkin' like a white boy." They jeered my dress, my grades, and my respect for the teachers and administrators—almost everything about me.

My only friends were two white boys who I'm convinced were left back a couple of grades. They took a liking to me and figured I needed their help if I was going to make it through the school year without being beaten up. When my father returned from Thailand and we got our next duty assignment to Spain, I couldn't get out of there fast enough.

I've read a lot of studies and commentary suggesting that claims of black children dismissing academic achievement and proper speech among their peers—or accusing them of "acting white"—is a myth. You can throw all the numbers at me that you want, but you'll never convince me. I lived it for a year and it left an indelible impression on my young psyche.

We lived in Spain for more than three years and while my awareness of race was certainly greater, I don't recall a great deal of racial tension in the military community where we lived. My parents had plenty of black and white friends as they always did, and among their favorites was an interracial couple that lived across the street from us, a black airman and his white French wife—little did I know that I would be mirroring their relationship a decade later. I've read that racial tensions were a real problem in the U.S. Army during the 1970s, but it didn't seem to be nearly as great an issue in the

Air Force, at least not to my knowledge. We left Spain in 1975 with my idealism relatively intact.

The next stop for us and my dad's last duty assignment before his retirement from the Air Force was Abilene, Texas. This was the first time other than our occasional stops in Louisiana where I went to school outside the base, and the difference was immediately apparent to me. Divisions by race and class were pretty common, although there were rarely any incidents. I was a novelty to my white friends and black students generally ignored me unless they needed my help with school assignments or they were involved in the Junior ROTC program as I was.

Most of the race-based incidents I experienced in my junior and senior year of high school revolved around dating, a topic that gets a chapter of its very own. Beyond that, I don't recall race being a dominant issue and, when it did come up, it was usually in a humorous vein.

Of interest was the general perception my white friends had of me. They often told me they didn't think of me as black. I know some blacks who are uncomfortable with such a statement because they don't like the suggestion that they are separate or distant from the black community, or they resent it because they think it reflects the low expectations of those making the statement and their pleasant surprise at being proved wrong.

For me, it was a triumph because I believed our goal was to stand out not because of our race, but rather our uniqueness of personality. I thought being recognized as a person first was the realization of Dr. Martin Luther King's dream that we would "one day live in a nation where they [his children] will not be judged by the color of their skin, but by the content of their character." Ironically, in my day-to-day interaction with the world, the people calling attention to my race were usually black, not white.

Through my college years, my race was mostly a novelty rather than a nuisance because of the unusual combination of my skin color, diction, deportment, and the political beliefs I held. I remember three experiences: one of which I could clearly categorize as racial discrimination and the other two which were less clear but suspicious to me in hindsight.

Perhaps the most blatant act of racism that personally affected me occurred as I was preparing to graduate from Texas Tech University in Lubbock, Texas. I was a summer graduate with a reporting date to the U.S. Air Force still several months away. I also wanted to participate in the graduation procession, something that wasn't done in the summer and for which I'd have to wait until the end of the fall semester.

Given that fact, I planned to hang around Lubbock for the fall term even though I was no longer taking classes, and that meant moving out of the private dormitory where I lived and into an apartment. For financial reasons, I decided to share an apartment with a platonic female friend who was also black.

My friend had learned about some new apartments opening up not far from campus, so she decided to go check them out. She came back and told me they had sold out. Since the ads mentioning the availability of units for rent had just been posted, that seemed suspicious to us.

A couple of girls we knew from the Texas Tech Air Force ROTC program, both of whom happened to be white, agreed to go to the apartment complex and see if the manager offered to show them a place for rent. Sure enough, they reported back that he showed them several available units and gave them a contract to review and sign. Just to confirm our suspicions, my black female friend went back that same day and was told again that there was, metaphorically, no room in the inn.

Once we concluded they were discriminating against us because of race, we acted quickly. We reported the apartment complex to the university and threatened to report them to the housing authorities at nearby Reese Air Force Base, potentially shutting them off from hundreds of military apartment seekers.

The owner of the apartment complex immediately apologized and blamed the incident on a site manager who was subsequently fired. We were offered the opportunity to look at their available rentals, but we had since made other arrangements.

For a lot of blacks, this would have been another brick in the wall of racial separation between blacks and whites in America. For me, it was an isolated incident that we reported promptly and which was handled swiftly and to my satisfaction. The system worked.

An earlier episode was not an obvious case of racial discrimination, but it was suspicious to my girlfriend at the time and to me in retrospect. I interviewed for a job at a popular bar and grill across the street from campus. The hiring manager seemed very positive about bringing me on board as a greeter and order taker because he liked how I presented myself. I was promptly hired and, for the first week, I greeted patrons as they came into the establishment and I took their orders.

After only one week and without warning or an explanation, I was ordered back into the kitchen to prepare food. I dutifully obeyed but hated the work, especially making onion rings because the smell of onions was nearly impossible to scrub off of my hands and stayed with me for weeks.

My girlfriend suspected the reason I was "demoted" without warning or apparent cause was because some patron didn't like seeing a black man at the front counter. I scoffed at the idea but couldn't come up with anything better. Not long afterwards, I was fired from the job for calling in sick. That stunned me. I had never called in sick before and was always on time and fulfilled all hours when I worked.

When I called in, my boss threatened me with termination if I didn't come in. I begged for his consideration because I was genuinely ill and, not only did I need to recover, I didn't think I should be preparing food. I didn't report to work and, true to his word, he fired me. I'm sure there were a hundred other college students lined up to take my place, so he had no qualms about his decision. To this day, I don't really know what happened there and my girlfriend's suggestion is the only thing that seems to make sense.

Still, it was a onetime setback, not a permanently debilitating experience, so I brushed it off, went about my business and found another job.

Preceding even these episodes was something that happened to me at the U.S. Military Academy at West Point, an institution I should never have attended. I made an impulsive decision on the day of my high school graduation to accept an appointment to West Point based on the history and prestige of the institution, along with its sterling track record of developing our nation's leaders. I thought it was destiny calling. Instead, I was ill-prepared for the experience, it backfired on me and messed me up for the rest of my days in college.

I already knew the entrenched attitudes at West Point included a tendency toward discrimination. My class was the second to admit women to the academy, so we were the first "plebe" (freshman) class to deal with upper class female cadets.

To me, there was no issue. In the West Point culture, plebes were no better than debris on the bottom of a more senior cadet's shoe and we were to obey all lawful orders given to us by upper class cadets regardless of gender.

The upper class male cadets had different ideas. They actively encouraged plebes not to obey orders from their female counterparts. I also thought the women in our class were singled out for particularly harsh treatment. Many very bright and dedicated women left or were forced into circumstances that led to their dismissal. It was unfair and it was wrong.

One late fall afternoon just before dinner, I was summoned to an upperclassman's room and told to wear full marching gear. I reported with rifle in hand and was immediately "braced" up against the upperclassman's wardrobe closet. From that moment forward, I was subjected to a lengthy period of hazing by that upperclassman and another who joined him.

By 1977, hazing was not officially tolerated at West Point, but that didn't stop it. Few of us had experienced it and I don't remember all the details of what happened to me. I do remember being terrified as those two upperclassmen stood about an inch from my face and screamed insults at the top of their lungs for what seemed like an eternity.

They forced me to pull my head into my neck and try to squeeze my chin inside my collar. I was ridiculed for being "soft" and I seem to recall some offensive comments about my mother. They let me go just before dinner assembly and I remember going back to my room, hurling my rifle onto the bed in frustration and trying to dry my tears before going to formation.

While at dinner, I was approached by one of the cadet officers and, as I sat at attention as plebes were required to do, he quietly spoke an apology for what had happened to me and told me the two upperclassmen were out of line. Others came forward and offered words of support, so it lifted my spirits considerably.

What does this have to do with race? Well, I was the only black cadet in my company and these two upperclassmen were from Arkansas and Alabama, respectively. Add to that the general opinion within my company that I wasn't a "strack trooper," meaning a person exhibiting exceptional military appearance and the highest standards of dress, or "gung-ho." I was a quiet, bookish and sheltered teenager who had never been away from home before. So I was an inviting target for harassment.

Looking back on it, I wondered if the apparent embarrassment exhibited by the upper class cadets at the behavior of their contemporaries was because their motives weren't pure, i.e., they were racially motivated.

I'll never know. Subsequently, they harassed me again, not as severely as the first time but still without cause in my opinion. However, when I reported it, I was the one subjected to criticism for my actions. The first time, I remained silent and it was the grapevine that spread the news and led to the expressions of sympathy from the cadet leadership.

Frustrated by the artificial stress and mind games at West Point, I concluded that I went to college to get an education, not to be harassed. Therefore, I left after only seven months and 22 days. (But who was counting?) It was my first significant failure and my parents were displeased, especially my father, who didn't speak to me for months afterwards.

When I finally confronted him about his silence, he told me he was disappointed in me because he believed I could do anything I set my mind to. He said my failure wasn't because I couldn't do it, but I chose not to do it. It wasn't until I graduated and received my Air Force commission that he was proud of me once again.

My self-esteem took a major hit because of my West Point experience and I struggled through what should have been a cakewalk at Texas Tech. My grades were only average and if I overachieved as an Air Force officer, part of it was to convince myself that I was still capable of excellence.

Once I was on active duty with the Air Force, it was like coming home again. Everything I remember that was positive about the armed forces, specifically its integrated communities and lifestyle, and its emphasis on proper race relations during our training, education and professional development, was still in place and had become well established over more than two decades.

I came to believe, and still do today, that the U.S. military is the closest thing to a meritocracy. After all, accomplishing the mission is the singular most important goal and since racism is contrary to mission accomplishment, good order among the troops is required.

In fact, I felt that being black and highly competent was a career advantage for me because my superiors had someone who could help them score diversity points in their officer evaluations. But in me, they also had someone who could perform the tasks at hand with distinction.

My Air Force career was, in a word, outstanding. I was going through my Air Force personnel file while doing research for this book, and the awards, commendations, "firewall" evaluations and letters of appreciation from generals, foreign officers and senior civilian officials prompted me to say to myself, "This guy was pretty amazing—I wonder what happened to him?" My wry observation was made somewhat in jest, but my nearly nine-and-a-half-year Air Force career represented the longest sustained stretch of outstanding performance in my professional life to date.

While I believed the combination of my race, demeanor and communication skills opened many doors for me during my Air Force career, I know of many other black officers who believed they were subjected to subtle racial discrimination in career advancement and assignment opportunities. They declared racial discrimination an institutional problem rather than a series of uncharacteristic or isolated incidents. I don't doubt the sincerity of their beliefs, I just never witnessed or experienced it myself.

I struggled with their claims of discrimination because if it were a systemic problem, why wasn't I experiencing it as well? I didn't assume it was a performance issue. As far as I could tell, these black officers were outstanding performers. Was I so naïve? Was racism occurring around me and I didn't recognize it? And if it really existed but had no discernible impact on my advancement or my working relationships with my superiors, peers and subordinates, did it matter?

Outside of work, I recall a couple of annoying incidents that took place in Florida while out on my morning run. In one instance, I encountered an elderly man with a walking stick approaching me as I ran on the sidewalk. As we drew closer, he began swinging his walking stick back and forth, and kept doing it as I ran past him. Once I passed him, I looked behind me and he had stopped swinging his stick. Apparently, he thought I was a threat and was making those menacing moves as some kind of warning to me. Over time, he realized I was no threat to him, so he ceased swinging the only weapon he had in hand.

The other incident occurred as I was doing my cooldown walk. I came up behind a couple of women walking together, both of them white. I couldn't help but notice they kept looking back at me as if they were expecting me to attack them. Eventually, I came to my house and peeled off in that direction. We owned one of the newest and largest homes in the neighborhood, and I felt like shouting after these women, "You see this big, beautiful house here? I own it!"

There might have been other slurs and slights directed at me in my lifetime because of race, but the incidents I've cited above are the only ones I recall. I didn't have the cumulative experiences that led me to the conclusion reached by so many of my black colleagues that America is a nation hopelessly hindered by race. That probably made it easier for me to dismiss episodes like these as aberrations rather than indicators of a systemic problem.

With limited exposure to racism and its effects, the unique upbringing of military life, only an academic awareness of and practically no personal experience with the civil rights movement, and a guileless and congenial personality that extends to everyone the presumption of good faith, if there is a racist America that exists all around me, I am mercifully unaware of or unaffected by it.

I didn't experience the struggles of the civil rights movement and consider myself a beneficiary of its triumphs. When I've experienced racially-motivated setbacks, I've dealt with them individually and left them in the past. In short, I have had a blessed life.

In the minds of most black Americans, however, the arc of my life and the conclusions I've reached disqualify me from speaking on matters of race.

Since my intent is not to disparage the experiences of others, I've struggled to determine what factors have largely shielded me from the scourge of racism that apparently has adversely affected other blacks. Is it gullibility on my part? Am I being manipulated? Is there something about my behavior or demeanor that elicits a different, positive reaction from whites? Is it the positive expectation with which I generally approach the world?

I find the experiences of African immigrants in America to be instructive. To a typical white person, there is no visual difference between a black American and an African immigrant. If racism were deeply ingrained in American culture, its adverse effects should conceivably have an impact on all blacks regardless of origin.

Africans have the highest levels of educational attainment of any immigrant group, exceeding even Asian-Americans who are stereotyped as being exceptionally well-educated. In fact, Africans are more highly educated than any native-born ethnic group, including white

Americans. A higher percentage of African immigrants have graduate degrees than white or black Americans. African immigrants are wealthier than black Americans too.

I would argue that if racism is omnipresent throughout American society, and the primary cause of black social ills in this country, it's logical to assume African blacks would be struggling right alongside their black American counterparts. That doesn't appear to be the case, at least when it comes to two measures of success, educational attainment and wealth creation.

The two conclusions one can reach about race in America are diametrical opposites. Either there is systemic racism and all are affected by it, whether or not they realize it, or racism is an occasional occurrence contingent on circumstances or expectations and it is propagated by individuals and not society at large.

In my opinion, the former makes no sense in the context of my personal ascendancy and that of millions of other blacks over the past 50 years. So the latter seems more consistent with my personal experiences than any other explanation I can divine.

Racism hasn't hindered me in the pursuit or achievement of my goals. Racism didn't stop me from attaining an education, finding and keeping a job, and marrying and raising a family, a sequence of actions which, if taken in that order, contribute more significantly to freedom from poverty than any government program. Racism doesn't take from me or anyone else the power to make the right personal choices.

Let me be clear: I'm not now, nor have I ever been, of the opinion that racism doesn't exist. As long as there is sin in the heart of man, racism will always be with us. It is how we respond when we encounter it that makes all the difference.

I remember a saying that Rev. Jesse Jackson used to make during many of his public appearances:

"Excellence is the best deterrent to racism." In other words, don't get mad or get even. Get better. Every time we fall short of excellence, we figuratively give racists the rope with which to hang us.

Racism is predicated on the alleged superiority of one race over another, but every man or woman of the presumably inferior race that achieves excellence exposes racism for the lie it is.

Excellence also confounds those who would attempt to use race against you. To quote the old English proverb, "Living well is the best revenge."

The other pearl of wisdom I always carry with me came from my father. I asked him why he seemed to have no animus or resentment toward whites, despite growing up in the South during the Jim Crow era.

My father was a quiet man, so when he spoke, his words carried a lot of meaning. He paused, took stock of my question and said, "I always figured you catch more flies with honey than vinegar."

My father chose not to let racism have any power over him and it's a lesson I've taken to heart. Subsequently, I learned his approach was entirely Biblical. In his letter to the church in Rome, St. Paul provided the perfect blueprint for confronting evil, and racism is certainly evil:

> *Never pay back evil for evil to anyone. Respect what is right in the sight of all men. If possible, so far as it depends on you, be at peace with all men. Never take your own revenge, beloved, but leave room for the wrath of God, for it is written, "Vengeance is Mine, I will repay," says the Lord. "But if your enemy is hungry, feed him, and if he is thirsty, give him a drink; for in so doing you will heap burning coals on his head." Do not be overcome by evil, but overcome evil with good.*[o]

---

[o] Romans 12:17-21.

The prevailing attitude today among Americans in general and blacks in particular is not to let anyone "disrespect" you and to retaliate at any perceived slight. We're also encouraged to have long memories and forgiveness is largely unheard of.

Regardless of our individual or collective history or experiences, God's advice for human relations should prevail. He created us and wrote the owner's manual.

He says to forgive and forget transgressions against us as He forgives and forgets our transgressions. He admonishes us to leave vengeance to Him, so we're to respond to evil with good. He promises that our enemies will experience a burning remorse when their evil is met with good.

We can't control the actions of society toward us, but we can control our actions toward society. At the end of the day, the only way we're going to make race irrelevant is to start living that way and not wait for society to get its act together.

William Raspberry, the nationally syndicated columnist and author, spoke of the manner in which he deals with racism. The positive outcome of his approach mirrors my own:

The truth is, for me, I have almost all of my life been more attuned to opportunities than to barriers. It's the opportunity that attracted my attention. When you focus merely on the reality of the problem, if you're not careful, it will impede your progress. If you focus on the opportunity, you learn how to take what you have and make of it what you need. It's about accepting a wider reality that racism surely exists, but opportunity also exists. Because it has worked for me, I find myself focusing on the opportunity side. I've seen colleagues lose their jobs or suffer from racism, and honestly it hasn't happened much to me, or it has happened in episodes. A lot of my life has been an unplanned blessing, and for that, I'm grateful.[20]

Trials of Many Kinds

*Consider it all joy, my brethren, when you encounter
various trials, knowing that the testing of your faith
produces endurance. And let endurance have its
perfect result so that you may be perfect and complete,
lacking in nothing. But if any of you lacks wisdom,
let him ask of God, who gives to all generously
and without reproach, and it will be given to him.*
~ The Letter of James, 1:2-5

One of the reasons, perhaps the primary reason, that racism hasn't been a hindrance in my life is because I believe in a purposeful God Who's bigger than racism and any other obstacle that attempts to prevent me from realizing His plan. I find great strength and serenity in my favorite Bible verse: "'For I know the plans that I have for you,' declares the LORD, 'plans for welfare and not for calamity to give you a future and a hope.'"[p]

I am convinced that, as long as I stay in the center of God's will, He will honor His promises. He fills His Word with encouragement and assurances that nothing, not even the evil of racism, will stay His hand:

*What then shall we say to these things? If God is
for us, who is against us? (Romans 8:31)*

---

[p] Jeremiah 29:11.

And we know that God causes all things to work together for good to those who love God, to those who are called according to his purpose. (Romans 8:28)

No weapon that is formed against you will prosper... (Isaiah 54:17)

For nothing will be impossible with God. (Luke 1:37)

The confidence that God gives me to let no man stand between me and His purpose has also gradually brought me back to my childhood assurance that my Christianity and my pursuit of political solutions to the problems of race are not separate endeavors. Indeed, everything I do should be infused with the imprint of Christ, because everything I am is due to the blood and salvation of Christ.

My dilemma, however, isn't just whether or not my passions of faith and politics can co-exist within me, but what that looks like in practice. It's the "how" that continues to task me. The assurances I had in 1969 have been challenged time and again by others. I have even questioned myself. It's been a lifelong quest to find God's place for me.

The first time this question of how to reconcile faith and politics really weighed on me was when I returned to the church in 1992. Up until that time, I had no doubt that my future would be in politics. My political activities in college could have led to me running for the Texas legislature after graduation, but I had a four-year Air Force commitment to fulfill.

I couldn't be politically active while in the Air Force, but in 1990 I did engage in one major civic activity. I collaborated with my former Air Force colleague, Mark Solomon, on a position paper called "An Experiment in Democracy" and the goal was to send it to several members of the U.S. Congress, even the vice president of the United States, to see how many would respond to two ordinary citizens petitioning their government.

Not surprisingly, we didn't get many responses and most of those we received were form letters. We sent some copies of the paper to a few press people and their reaction caught us by surprise. Before long, my friend and I were doing a radio show in Seattle, and I was on TV in Melbourne, Florida to discuss the paper. Nationally syndicated columnist David Broder even wrote about it, calling the paper "exceptionally clear and compelling."

The interesting thing was that my friend and I were on opposite sides of the aisle politically. He was a Democrat and I a Republican. We collaborated on the contents, I wrote the paper and the positions we took were strictly middle of the road. At that time, I wasn't practicing my faith and anyone who would read the paper today would be surprised to see my name attached to it. It wasn't necessarily controversial, it just didn't reflect the world-view I now hold. I don't know if my friend and I could collaborate on a similar project today.

The notoriety the paper brought us, however, stirred my political juices and not long after that, I made the decision to separate from the Air Force and return to civilian life so I could lay the groundwork for reentering the political arena.

A couple of things happened to change my plans. The first was the realization that I still had a family to feed, shelter and clothe. Considering my duty as the husband of Annik and the father of my children, I wasn't going to chase rainbows without ensuring their stability and security. That meant giving most of my attention when away from home to my job as a contractor hired by the U.S. Air Force. The other thing that happened was—well—God.

I mentioned in an earlier chapter that my grandfather died unexpectedly and his death was the catalyst for bringing me back to Christ. However, my return to the church seriously complicated things for me. All I wanted to do was God's will, so I questioned everything I held dear prior to my recommitment to Christ, including my political ambitions. I had to examine whether they were a product of God's leading or my own earthly desires.

My rise in politics, beginning with my job at the tender age of 18 as a researcher and speechwriter for a candidate seeking a seat in Congress, through my activities at Texas Tech, to the position paper I'd written a year earlier, wasn't influenced by my faith. For over a decade, very little in my life had been influenced by my faith.

Everything changed after I let Christ back into my life and I remember long discussions with my pastor about my calling and how conflicted I was about my future, something I'd never experienced before. Years later, after I moved to the Washington, DC area, he told me he never doubted that my calling was in the public arena, but I had to reach that conclusion on my own. But I'm getting ahead of myself.

These conflicts and the lack of opportunities to reenter politics led me to become fully immersed in the church, which offered the perfect outlet for my utmost desire, Christ. I sang on the church praise team and choir because music is a vocation that has held me lovingly and willingly captive since I was an 11 year old in the Sunbeam Choir at Mount Calvary Baptist Church. I taught Sunday school and served on the building committee, pouring myself into the church with great vigor and happiness.

I sniffed politics again briefly when I single-handedly and successfully lobbied the Melbourne City Council to issue business licenses to home-based businesses. There I learned a couple of things from the experience. One is that a well prepared and persistent advocate can go far in making change in the government, especially at the local level.

The other thing I learned is how condescending and arrogant our elected officials are toward the people who elected them. I never forgot how indignant I was when certain so-called public servants mistreated me and other taxpaying citizens. That has influenced my attitude about the proper "positional relationship," to borrow a phrase from my pastor, between the elected official and those who elected them. Thus, if I'm ever in a position to make something happen, my goal is to reestablish, through word and deed, the elected official as a servant leader who owes the people industry, experience and respect.

By the time we moved to Tampa in 1998, I was pretty convinced that a life in politics was not in the cards for me. I recall making contact with an old Air Force colleague who was living in Austin, Texas and finding out that he was working in the Office of the Texas Attorney General, serving then-Governor George W. Bush.

It was quite a turn of events because when we were stationed together, my friend and I shared a common interest in politics, and I'd regale him with stories of my campaign experiences, including my brief stint as a volunteer for George W. Bush's first political campaign. Little did I imagine that, years later, my friend would be working for Bush at the highest levels of state government and I'd be doing the daily grind, commuting to and from an uninspiring job that paid the bills and offered little else.

Things changed a few days before the 2000 general election, when my friend sent me an email declaring he had been tabbed for the Bush Administration transition team should the governor win the election for president. He also said that Bush's election was practically a certainty. So he asked me to consider, after prayer and reflection, whether I would be interested in serving in the new administration.

At the very time in my life when I had given up on the possibility of ever serving in a political capacity, when I had been reduced to gazing wistfully at friends traveling down the path I once thought was also mine, a door was opened for me. I told my friend that yes, I'd be honored to serve the new president.

As it turned out, there was the minor hiccup of a contested election that ended only when the Supreme Court stepped in and brought a halt to the process, thereby clearing the way for Gov. Bush to become president.

On the personal front, my excitement at the possibility of working in Washington, DC was tempered by practical considerations. Could we afford to live in so expensive an area? What if the position I'm offered doesn't pay enough for me and my family to subsist?

My mind swirled with questions as I was driving to work one morning and I whispered a prayer to God to show me the answers. All of a sudden, I felt an eerie sense of calm wash over me and my mind was invaded by the words "I will be with you." It was a supernatural experience and I felt much more at peace about the entire situation after that.

The interview process in Washington was frustrating at first. As I walked into the White House office of my friend, by then an associate counsel to the president, I wondered if I had deceived myself yet again.

My friend and I had served together as intelligence officers before he left active duty, got a law degree and began his new career as an advocate. He and his associates in the White House personnel office had been targeting me toward intelligence positions, but that wasn't working out. The Washington intelligence community is pretty close-knit and change occurs primarily at the highest levels, where politics is as much a deciding factor as experience, so those positions were mostly filled.

It didn't help that I'd been out of the operational intelligence business for a few years. Even though my work after the Air Force involved providing support to military intelligence organizations, it was mostly in the information technology arena. By the time my friend extended to me the offer to interview for a political appointment, I was no longer supporting intelligence organizations and was a project manager for a professional services firm.

It was that background that led the White House personnel office to suggest I interview for some information technology posts they were having trouble filling. As I sat in my friend's office discussing this change in direction, I noticed a book on his desk, *The Prayer of Jabez* by Bruce H. Wilkinson. I'd heard about it. It was a best-selling book at the time, but the fuss over it seemed a little faddish to me. My friend said someone had given it to him and I was welcome to it if I wanted it. I was curious enough to accept his offer.

I was staying with my best friend from my earliest days in the Air Force. He and his family live in a beautiful suburban county about 45 miles southeast of Washington. This friend was optimistic that I'd get a political appointment because he, too, knew of my passion for politics and was convinced that this was the opportunity I'd been waiting for all my life. So while I stayed with him and tried to determine my professional future, he urged me to move to Calvert County, Maryland once I was hired. Still, I wasn't as convinced as he was. All I knew was that I had a lot of decisions to make and nothing to hang my hat on just yet.

As I lay in the guest bedroom, I read the book my friend had given me from cover to cover. It was a short and therefore a quick read, and it told the story of Jabez, a character in the book of 1 Chronicles who prayed a prayer to be richly blessed and had his prayer answered. The name "Jabez" sounds like the Hebrew word for pain and the fact that there is a reference to his mother but not his father suggests a difficult upbringing. So the answer to his prayer illustrated the overcoming of adversity and the wisdom of petitioning God boldly for what we desire. Jabez also stood out because the author saw fit to mention him prominently amid a listing of great kings and their lineage. The passage in 1 Chronicles[q] that describes Jabez is brief:

Jabez was more honorable than his brothers, and his mother named him Jabez saying, "Because I bore him with pain."

Now Jabez called on the God of Israel, saying, "Oh that You would bless me indeed and enlarge my border, and that Your hand might be with me, and that You would keep me from harm that it may not pain me!" And God granted him what he requested.

Wilkinson argues that God wants to release great blessings into the lives of those who love Him and seek to do His will, but they must approach God with boldness and ask Him to enlarge their borders. He cited the power of this prayer in his own life and the lives of others, and encourages his readers to pray the prayer just as Jabez did.

I'll admit I was skeptical. In the meantime, I've learned that the author's theology and his highly successful marketing of *The Prayer of Jabez* aren't universally accepted. After all, critics claim, God isn't a holy ATM machine where we put in our requests and He dispenses our wishes accordingly.

Still, I knew the verse in the Letter of James that says, "You do not have because you do not ask."[r] I understood that in petitioning God, it is His will be done, not mine. Therefore, if He would enlarge my territory, it would be

---

[q] 1 Chronicles 4:9-10.

[r] James 4:2.

to His glory. I discerned that even though God already knows the desires of our hearts, He wants us to speak them to Him because He desires to be in relationship with us. As far as these theological truths are concerned, Dr. Wilkinson's teaching was spot on.

I also realized that I'd recited the Lord's Prayer all my life without questioning it as a petition, so I saw the prayer of Jabez as no different. So, in the bedroom of my friend's home, I tentatively dropped to my knees and, taking the prayer into my heart and making it mine, I spoke it aloud to the Lord. Then I went to sleep wondering what the days to come would bring.

I was scheduled for two interviews the next day before flying back to Florida, one with the deputy chief of staff at the Federal Emergency Management Agency (FEMA) and another with an official at the Department of Defense. The FEMA interview started out with the deputy chief of staff asking questions while he changed clothes for another meeting—his office attire consisted of flip-flops and no tie. The first question he asked me was, "Why is a black dude like you a Republican?" I knew this was going to be an unconventional interview. Still, his directness and casual demeanor relaxed me and what was supposed to be a half-hour interview ended up taking an hour and a half. As I was walking out the door, he told me not to make a commitment to any other agency without talking to him first.

The interview at the Department of Defense was more formal but went equally well. The hiring manager and the interviewer were both impressed with me and said I was the kind of person they needed. I left there for the airport and, as I prepared to board the plane, I realized that I had gone, in less than 24 hours, to having no prospects at all to having two good ones. I looked at the small book in my hands and a stupid grin crossed my face, a grin that comes to me whenever God's faithfulness is explicitly revealed to me.

The Jabez story doesn't end there. A few weeks later, I flew back to Washington to interview with the director of FEMA, Joe Allbaugh. While in flight, I re-read *The Prayer of Jabez* once more to remind myself of the teaching therein and I silently recited the prayer. A flight attendant noticed the book and remarked that she'd heard a lot about it and hoped to buy a copy someday. As we de-boarded the plane, I handed her my copy of the book and wished her well.

My interview with Director Allbaugh went well, but he said he wanted to think about it some more. I set my things in an empty office where I would wait until the time came for me to depart for my flight. Then I went to lunch. Upon my return, the FEMA chief of staff asked me to review an important document and offer my opinion. I agreed and began flipping through the pages. The chief of staff brought in another person to meet me and she introduced me as "the new IT guy." She then took me to the human resources department and, after that, the IT department. Everyone was reacting to me as if I'd already been hired.

It turns out that I was hired and didn't know it. After the interview concluded and I went to lunch, the chief of staff, deputy chief of staff and general counsel had gone into Allbaugh's office and essentially told him, "You gotta hire this guy!" By the time I came back and the chief of staff handed me the document to review, I'd gotten the job!

As I prepared to depart, Allbaugh stuck his head out of his office, spotted me and asked, "Can you be here in two weeks?" I stammered a "Yes, sir" and left with my head swimming. I had so much to do when I returned home—quit my job, put the house up for sale, say farewell to my church family—and so little time.

I made arrangements to stay with my friends in Calvert County until our house sold and we were able to buy a home in our new home state. I started work on June 4, 2001, exactly two weeks after my interview and as Director Allbaugh had requested. I was the chief information officer (CIO) in waiting for FEMA.

The "in waiting" part was because my predecessor was still in place, a luxury for me because I had the benefit of his knowledge and experience for the next four months. In the meantime, I was made the deputy CIO even though the person occupying that chair had yet to retire. He graciously stepped aside and also offered his help toward a smooth transition. I looked forward to easing into my new role gradually and quietly.

My expectations were dramatically altered on the morning of September 11, 2001. I was in a hotel room in Big Sky, Montana, having arrived at the ski resort the night before to be introduced that morning to the National Emergency Management Association (NEMA) as FEMA's new CIO. While I was getting ready, I turned on the television and flipped to CNN, my channel of choice when I travel.

The commentators suddenly broke away to show one of the towers of New York City's World Trade Center with a huge gash in its side, black smoke billowing from it. The initial reports suggested a Cessna or other light plane might have inadvertently strayed into restricted airspace and slammed into the building. I recall one of the experts they consulted by phone, a former National Transportation Safety Board official, declaring ominously that, and I'm paraphrasing, "This was no accident. The airspace is restricted for a mile around the Twin Towers."

Right at that moment, a huge fireball erupted from the other tower and I remember jumping up from the bed and running as fast as I could to get to the ballroom where the NEMA conference was being held. Director Allbaugh, his press secretary, and a host of others were rushing to their cars to get to the airport at nearby Bozeman. Someone yelled on the way out the door that a military transport would be sent to pick up the rest of us.

In the meantime, I got to work trying to get us connected to the internet so we could do our jobs from the hotel ballroom, which was instantly transformed from a meeting place into a command center. The hotel staff had no networking equipment I could use, so I plugged a laptop into the nearest phone wall jack, grabbed an internet connection and didn't let it go for the rest of the day.

That turned out to be a wise move, since the telephone lines were saturated and we weren't able to call into Washington, DC. As far as communications were concerned, I was the only conduit back to FEMA. Our public affairs people were bringing me press releases to send out and others were handing me items of importance to communicate back to headquarters. I also contacted state officials with the Montana National Guard to make arrangements for a secure phone system to be delivered to us.

I remember sitting at a table helping people get their messages out while the events of the day as reported by CNN were being projected onto a large screen or wall near where I sat. We were hearing rumors that the Capitol or the White House had been hit, that a car bomb had gone off in the State Department parking lot, and that Washington was in total gridlock. While only the last report was true, many of us were frightened for our families and friends back home. All of us watched in stunned silence at the large projected image as the Twin Towers collapsed. Many wept.

A fellow FEMA associate director, a former Marine, remarked that what we were seeing was the beginning of a war and I wondered how many other targets there were across the country. Our hotel was on total lockdown with local law enforcement surrounding our building and preventing movement between buildings on the resort campus.

I prayed that no one I knew from my days in the military or as a defense contractor was in the section of the Pentagon that had been hit by American Airlines Flight 77. My family was 45 miles south of the Capitol, so I presumed they were safe. All we could do was to wait for the military transport that was supposed to come and get us.

Except it never came. The nation's airspace had been closed down and we were resigned to being where we were for a while. The days that followed were spent monitoring news reports and communicating with staff back at FEMA, checking in on family members and assuring other family and friends that I wasn't in Washington, DC and was, in fact, okay.

I called my pastor from our church in Tampa and he asked to do an interview with me about the horrific events of the past few days so that he could share it with the congregation. I agreed and during the interview I reminded whoever would be listening that God was in control—even though it didn't seem that way. God especially cared for the nearly 3,000 people murdered by terrorists, and the family and friends they left behind. I prayed a lot.

Some people were getting the ski resort equivalent of cabin fever and couldn't wait for the airspace to reopen, so they rented a car and drove back to Washington, DC. I declined, confident that the airspace would soon be reopened and I would be home before they would. My prediction proved to be correct and I didn't have to endure days on the road to get home.

It was while preparing to board the flight at the Bozeman airport that I realized life would never be the same again. The airport screeners were opening up and checking all luggage, screening each passenger for possible weapons, and the long line of people didn't seem to mind. Everyone was quiet and serious while they waited. It was a grim but determined people I saw that day.

The air traffic control system was chaotic that day after four days without flights, and our flight was diverted to Minneapolis, then Pittsburgh. I finally arrived at Baltimore-Washington International early Saturday morning and had a quiet drive home.

My wife was still up when I got home and we were glad to be in each other's arms again. I could sense the concern inside her and was again reminded of how much had changed. Even though it was around 2 AM when I got home, I got some rest, cleaned up and drove into Washington, DC that afternoon to get right back to work.

The weeks that followed were filled with long hours and a lot of contingency planning since we thought another attack was imminent. I had prayed for God to enlarge my territory, and my prayers had been answered, although not in the way I expected. God never works in the way we hope or expect—that's why He's God and we're not.

I went from being just another federal senior executive to a key player in the government's fight against terrorism. FEMA was at the epicenter of emergency management for natural disasters, but now we added terrorism to the mix and elevated it to the top priority.

Information was critical to our emergency management and other national security missions, so I found myself attending numerous White House task force meetings, briefing members of Congress during testimony on Capitol Hill, interacting with other federal agencies and IT companies on warning systems and continuity of operations after a terrorist attack and so much more.

I was attending a lot of conferences and public events since Director Allbaugh, who was more of a doer than a talker, shunned them and sent me in his place instead. He told me once, as we were walking together to Capitol Hill to testify on an emergency management bill under consideration in the Senate, "I'm going to make you a star."

I couldn't tell if he was joking or not because his expression almost never changed, but I knew he liked and trusted me, and he supported every one of my initiatives to make FEMA better. My profile in the Washington, DC technology community, and the fledgling homeland security infrastructure that sprung up after 9/11, was extremely high. Consequently, a local technology magazine called me "one of the most visible CIOs in Washington."

One evening, Director Allbaugh asked me to attend a holiday reception in his stead to accept an award that FEMA was to receive for their efforts in the aftermath of 9/11. The reception turned out to be the NBC News annual holiday party. I called home and told Annik to buy herself a new outfit because we were going out on the town that evening.

While others were pulling up to the valet parking drop-off point in BMWs, Mercedes and Lexus sedans or sports coupes, we pulled up in our Dodge Caravan with the roller hockey gear in the back. We went into the posh hotel lobby where the reception was being held and no one paid us any attention. I pointed out to Annik people that I'd seen only on television like Tim Russert, Andrea Mitchell and her husband, Federal Reserve Chairman Alan Greenspan. It was pretty heady stuff for this son of an Air Force enlisted man and his teenage bride.

When the time came for me to accept the award on behalf of FEMA, the cameras all turned toward me and my wife. Flashbulbs were popping and people began to follow us wherever we went from that moment on. It was so humorous—one minute we were practically invisible, the next we were the center of attention. It was quite an introduction to Washington nightlife for the both of us and we had a splendid time.

To this day, being the FEMA CIO was the best job I've ever had. I had enormous responsibility in support of FEMA's mission to prepare for, prevent or respond to terrorist attacks or natural disasters. I had a boss who couldn't have been more supportive and public recognition as an important member of the homeland security community.

I also realized that all the jobs I'd held previously in the intelligence and IT professions—jobs which I thought had no relationship to my dreams of public service—actually had given me the skills and the confidence to do the work I was doing. I didn't see the connections, but God did.

I was amazed to see His plan come together and I gave Him the glory for my good fortune because He had shown me that "The mind of man plans his way, but the LORD directs his steps."[s] Little did I know that my trust in God's plan was about to be severely tested.

On the evening of June 6, 2002, two days after my first anniversary with FEMA, President Bush announced the creation of the Department of Homeland Security (DHS), the most ambitious reorganization of government since the National Security Act of 1947 which, among other things, created the Department of Defense and established the U.S. Air Force as a separate service. I was on travel, so Director Allbaugh called me earlier in the day to give me the news in advance of the president's address to the nation. He was convinced that FEMA was going to be the nucleus around which the new department was going to be built and he told me, "Your workload is about to increase."

I was a panelist at a homeland security conference in western Pennsylvania, as was Steve Cooper, the senior director and CIO for the White House Office of Homeland Security. The conference attendees were at dinner and

[s] Proverbs 16:9.

had a television in the room so we could watch when President Bush made his announcement. Steve and I were the only ones who knew what the president would announce and while we gave the people a heads-up to watch the speech, we didn't tell them what it was about.

Once President Bush had finished speaking, the others in the room immediately turned to us and bombarded us with questions. We really didn't know much more than what we'd all heard on television, but one question produced a particularly awkward moment. Someone asked, "So which one of you is going to be the new department's CIO?"

Steve and I looked at each other somewhat apprehensively. I let Steve, the more experienced of the two of us, answer the question. As I expected, he handled it very well, saying that such a decision was out of our hands and we'd be working together regardless of who filled that role. Nonetheless, the seed had been planted and the speculation became great sport in the federal technology community.

Washington, DC is a surreal world unto itself and things that consume government officials and federal workers have no parallel in the everyday world. Even though it's only 45 miles from Washington, DC, one of the blessings of living in Calvert County is that it's small-town America. To my family and friends, I wasn't some high and mighty federal official (and trust me, I didn't parade around like one!). I was simply Ron. That has helped me during some tough times in the nation's capital and I consider Calvert County to be my sanctuary from the distorted perspective of Washington, DC.

I mention this because in the weeks following President Bush's announcement, while millions of Americans were concerned about making a living and building their lives, Washington, DC was abuzz with speculation on who was going to be appointed to key positions in the new department.

Bringing over 20-plus federal agencies—the number changed frequently—and approximately 180,000 employees, not to mention facilities, contracts, private sector support, and all manner of resources, was an enormous undertaking. The positions in the new department were not only seen as plum jobs, but filling them would also result in others losing their current jobs. After all, the department only needed one of everything, right?

While I was secure in my role as the FEMA CIO and figured I'd have some role in the new department's information technology division, I was offered the opportunity to work with a transition planning team being set up by the White House. The Homeland Security Transition Planning Office (HSTPO) would undertake all the necessary steps to have the department operational as soon as possible after the legislation made it through Congress and was signed by the president.

I announced this at the morning staff meeting and Director Allbaugh, in a good mood since he had vacation time coming up, said mockingly, "Gee, I wonder how that happened." He then leaned over in his chair toward me and said, "I insisted on it!" I was relieved. I wanted to help the new department get started on the right foot, but I wanted his blessing first. Thinking I had it, I told Steve Cooper, the person who made the request to have me as his deputy in the HSTPO's Office of Information Programs, to proceed with the administrative steps necessary to make it happen.

Before he left for his vacation, Allbaugh called me into his office and announced he was raising my pay to bring me up to a level equivalent to other federal CIOs. He showered praise on me and told me he wished he could do more because he considered me a prized member of his staff.

Director Allbaugh was a gruff man and very hard to please. I'd seen him treat some of my colleagues pretty badly, but he had always been complimentary and supportive of me, so I didn't think much of anything about what had happened to others. The next meeting I'd have with him wouldn't take place for another two months.

Other FEMA staff members, notably the deputy director, Mike Brown, were also tapped for the HSTPO, and we were subsequently informed we were expected to devote full time to this new detail. I remember having several talks with Mike about the impact of this requirement on my current duties and I put together a contingency plan to keep things going forward.

I was very careful to keep Mike in the loop because he was my boss and he communicated regularly with Allbaugh, so he could keep him informed as well. As a former military officer, I was trained to use the chain of command and not go over my immediate supervisor to the senior official unless such official requested my presence. As I was to learn later, that was a mistake. FEMA isn't a military organization, nor were the two senior protagonists veterans who would have employed such a concept.

In early August, I took some vacation time so my family and I could visit relatives in Louisiana. While we were driving through western Virginia, I received an email message on my ever-present Blackberry from Steve that told me I was going to start work with the HSTPO immediately upon my return from leave.

I forwarded the message to Mike and my deputy at FEMA, Rose Parkes, so they would be ready to make the transition as we had discussed. Assured that I'd properly informed everyone, I took in the beauty of the Appalachian Mountains while my wife drove, and I drifted off to sleep.

Even on vacation, I was still on duty. My mother had scheduled for me to talk to a local TV station about my role at FEMA and, since it was hurricane season, how people in southwestern Louisiana could contact FEMA for assistance. On the drive home, we stopped off in Nashville because I had a convention to attend there. Upon our return home, I prepared myself mentally for the new challenge ahead of me.

I went into work and started handing off things to Rose. I prepared a briefing for the White House staff on the transition of some federal IT initiatives they had assigned to FEMA for which I was the senior leader. I got a phone call from a local government technology magazine that had heard rumors about my transfer to the HSTPO, so I confirmed the transfer and the handover of my daily FEMA duties to Rose Parkes for the near term. After that, all hell broke loose.

The new FEMA deputy chief of staff, a decidedly more formal person than the one who interviewed me the year before, called me into his office to relay his and Mike Brown's consternation at my "sudden" move to the HSTPO. I was confused. Had I been talking to myself for the past seven weeks? He then went on to detail issues that my peers had with my leadership of the IT department, our slow progress in modernizing FEMA's IT systems, and that I spent too much time traveling and speaking, and not enough doing my job.

This was all news to me. Just a few weeks prior, I was doing an excellent job, worthy of a significant pay increase—now this? I protested that change doesn't happen overnight and that we had to deal with passive resistance which slowed our progress.

I pointed out that my work with the White House on disaster management and emergency communications not only had Director Allbaugh's blessing, but was part of a larger strategy on my part to integrate FEMA's mission systems with these federal initiatives to help us secure funding and high-level support.

Moreover, since my trip to Montana on business the week of September 11, 2001, I hadn't traveled outside the DC area until April of 2002. So that charge was completely without merit.

It didn't seem to matter what I said. They had come up with a "story" about me. In Louisiana, if you're accused of "telling a story," that's another way of saying that you're lying. In Washington, once the story has been crafted and agreed upon, it becomes a narrative that is resistant to facts or rebuttal because there's an agenda behind it that's more important.

Subsequently, I went to my peers and asked which of them was dissatisfied with my work, but none would own up to making such a statement.

I told Rose, my deputy, that something was up and I wasn't sure what it was, but it didn't sound good. Not long after that, Mike found me at the HSTPO offices and told me he had spoken with Allbaugh, who was livid about what I had done.

I was confused and hurt. What was that whole act in the morning staff meeting where he claimed to have insisted on my being included on the transition team? Again, I went to my peers, asking them to validate what he had said in that meeting, but only one of them, the former Marine, corroborated my story. I felt like I was being railroaded and I still had no idea why.

I wasn't going to be able to speak with Allbaugh until his return in September and the notion of losing my biggest ally in Washington was disheartening. It made it very difficult for me to focus on the work I was selected to do.

The time finally came when he was back in town and I went to FEMA headquarters to meet with him. Mike told me he wanted to sit in on the meeting, which was my first sign that this wasn't going to be a pleasant experience.

The other was how the front office staff treated me when I arrived. They quickly ushered me into a spare office, ironically the same one where I found out I had been hired as the FEMA CIO. "Why can't I sit on the couch outside his office as I normally do?" I thought to myself.

As it turned out, he didn't have time to meet with me that day, so we had to reschedule for the following Monday. That stunk. It meant I'd be worrying the whole weekend away. I tried not to think about it. On Sunday, I took my seven-year-old son, Colin, to his first professional football game and we had a wonderful time. For a few hours, I felt human again.

Monday came and the long awaited meeting was finally going to happen. I figured I'd go in, explain the sequence of events, apologize for the misunderstanding and ask Director Allbaugh how he wanted me to proceed going forward. I never got the chance.

I opened my mouth and said, "Thank you for the opportunity to clear up this misunderstanding...," but he cut me off and said, "There is no misunderstanding. I'm relieving you of your duties as CIO effective immediately."

I was flabbergasted. I vaguely remember the rest of the meeting—accusations of betrayal, self-promotion and the biggest lie of all, that I'd done all of this surreptitiously, keeping everyone—even my own people—in the dark.

If there's one thing my people knew about me, it's that I communicated. In many cases, they'd probably say I communicated too much. I held more all-hands meetings with my people than any CIO before me and I even set aside an entire day where anyone could come into my office and talk about anything on their minds for 20 minutes. I learned a lot about the people working for me. I was even able to help a couple of female employees who weren't getting a fair shake when it came to promotion opportunities and better jobs.

I told the entire IT staff at an all-hands meeting before I departed for vacation that it was very possible

I'd be going to the HSTPO to work full-time and that I'd keep them informed. It was a bald-faced lie to say that my staff or anyone else that needed to know didn't know about it.

Allbaugh plunged the dagger deeper into my heart by saying he wished he'd never given me a pay raise, that I was trying to win favor with the White House and he was just giving me the opportunity to pursue what I really wanted. I recall muttering something about wanting his approval more than anything else and that if he'd told me to quit the HSTPO and devote myself exclusively to FEMA, I would've done so immediately.

All the while, Mike Brown just sat there, saying nothing. I felt like the victim of a violent crime, reaching out for help while a bystander watched and refused to get involved. Brown and Allbaugh had been friends since college, so he knew him as well as anyone. Why wasn't he defending me or telling him that his conclusions about me were all wrong?

Sometime later, Mike explained that he knew Allbaugh had already made up his mind and that, in a prior private conversation, Mike had talked him out of removing me from the FEMA payroll altogether, telling Allbaugh he'd be foolish to fire "an African-American and a devout Christian." I thought, that's something, I guess. But it brought me no solace. I was less concerned about the job and more concerned about the new distorted image he had of me, an image without a shred of truth in it.

I left the room shaken to my very core and the looks of sympathy from the front office staff just made me feel worse. I called my wife, informed Steve Cooper, and also called the former FEMA deputy chief of staff, who was genuinely surprised, even though I thought he was beyond surprise.

Steve was gracious and sent me home for the day. Since the next day was my daughter's 15th birthday, I decided to take that day off too.

As I drove home, I remember moaning, "Why, God? What did I do to deserve this?" The tears began to flow, but I squelched them immediately for the practical reason that I needed to be able to see in order to drive. The grief continued welling inside, but I decided to put off releasing it until I got home.

Annik and our children were determined not to let me wallow in my misery. As soon as I hit the door, they surrounded me with hugs and kisses and told jokes to make me laugh. The desire to cry went away and I never actually had the chance to mourn what had happened.

The rest of the year was a waste from my vantage point. I remember doing a previously scheduled panel in which I declared myself a failure for not meeting some of FEMA's greatest IT challenges and that ended up in the press as me criticizing FEMA. Allbaugh wanted to kick me off the FEMA payroll because of that, but Mike once again held him off, and I also had the White House staff looking out for me.

The opportunity arose for me to become the CIO at the Treasury Department, but that didn't come through. Steve, who by that time had been designated the first DHS CIO, promised to make me his deputy CIO when DHS went operational, but the incoming leadership dramatically reduced the number of senior executives he could have on his staff, declared he didn't need a deputy and, in the final blow to my hopes, said he couldn't have any political appointees on his staff. I had to go elsewhere.

The last time I saw Director Allbaugh was at a White House ceremony where the president recognized the leaders of the new department and lauded those assembled for their hard work in bringing it to fruition. At some point—I don't remember if it was before or after—I came across Allbaugh and Mike, who was slated to become the next director of FEMA and undersecretary for emergency preparedness. I reached out my hand to Allbaugh and he took it and said hello. That was about it.

Later, Mike mentioned to me that Allbaugh was boasting about shaking "that Ron Miller's hand" or words to that effect. I'm not sure why that was such a feat—as if I was untouchable or something. Despite all that had happened between us, I just wanted to demonstrate I could be civil when the occasion called for it.

The only highlight in the fall of 2002 was when I was one of a select few members of the HSTPO who were given an opportunity to meet the president. He personally thanked us for our help in establishing DHS.

I had spoken with President Bush briefly the year before when he visited FEMA. I thanked him for his faith in God and his response was that he couldn't do his job without Him. He didn't remember me from 24 years earlier when I had volunteered for his campaign in Lubbock, Texas, nor would I have expected him to.

We spent 45 minutes with President Bush in the Oval Office and he was a gracious, humble man who took his charge seriously, respected the dignity of his office and relied on prayer and God's Word to sustain him. I thought that if the American people could see him as we did at that meeting, they might not agree with him, but they would walk away respecting him. Looking back, I'm not so sure of that now. I wasn't familiar with Bush Derangement Syndrome at the time, but it was in full force already.

I had one more touch point with Director Allbaugh, although I never saw him again after that day outside the White House. I wrote him a note thanking him for giving me the opportunity to be the FEMA CIO, telling him it was the best job I ever had and asking his forgiveness if he felt betrayed by me because that was never my intent.

I don't know what prompted me to write the note. It was Christmastime and I guess I wanted to end things the right way. I also got him a book, *Jesus CEO* by Laurie Beth Jones, and told him he would find useful leadership advice through studying the life of Jesus.

I packaged the note and the book, gift wrapped it and delivered it to the FEMA front office for them to present to him. Not long after that, I received a very gracious note from him thanking me for the gift and wishing me well. I don't know if that constituted closure, but it was as close to it as I'd ever get.

He departed FEMA in March of 2003, and I asked Mike Brown, then in place as the director, if he minded me going to our remote location where most of the IT staff resided to hold a final all-hands meeting and bid them a proper farewell. He agreed, and I was able to thank them for what they'd done for me and tell them how much they meant to me.

A while after I'd left DHS, I had lunch with a former colleague of mine from FEMA, Anthony Lowe, a black attorney who Allbaugh hired to run FEMA's National Flood Insurance Program and its mitigation directorate. Anthony was one of the sharpest people I knew and he was a Washington veteran, having served as a legislative assistant for a U.S. congressman and senior legislative counsel for the Senate Judiciary Committee. It seemed, however, that he had recently run afoul of Director Allbaugh and his deputy chief of staff.

It was during that lunch that I shared my experiences with him. Until then, I had kept most of it to myself and only a small circle of people knew what had happened to me. After opening up to him, Anthony suggested that racism was at the heart of our troubles—after all, we were the only two black associate directors on Allbaugh's political staff.

I didn't think so. If Allbaugh were a racist, he wouldn't have appointed us in the first place. I didn't know the deputy chief of staff well enough to know whether or not he had an agenda, and to this day, I still don't have an explanation for what happened. I've tried not to speculate because it wouldn't change anything.

My last position in the Bush Administration was with the U.S. Small Business Administration (SBA), where I was responsible for helping them deliver as many of their small business products and services as possible over the internet. From the person that lured me there, I had a commitment of autonomy in my operations and a staff of people to help SBA "get to green" on the president's management scorecard for "e-government" initiatives.

I developed an organizational structure, defined the roles and responsibilities, and wrote the operations plan for approval by the leadership and, eventually, the Small Business Subcommittee in Congress. After the plan was approved and ready to go to Congress, I took some leave—I hadn't learned my lesson yet—and while I was out, they decided to scrap my plan and put me and my organization under another division.

The deputy chief of staff called me at home to ask if I was okay with it and since the SBA Administrator, Hector Barreto, had already signed off on their action before asking them to consult with me, my only choices were to say "No" and put myself at odds with the organization or accept what they'd already done. The conditions under which I agreed to go to SBA were no longer in place, but I had nowhere else to go.

I was miserable in my redefined role and treated with suspicion because of my previous bid for autonomy, so after a few months, I decided I would live up to my commitment to get SBA's e-government programs to "green," and then I was leaving government for good. In July of 2004, I bid the Bush Administration and all the hell it had put me through a bitter farewell.

Ironically, the people who brought me the most satisfaction in the three years I spent as a political appointee were the career civil servants, many of whom were hungry for reform and just needed someone to lead the way. Bush political appointees tended to keep the career workforce in the dark because they didn't trust them and that didn't go unnoticed.

I, on the other hand, considered them my teammates. I kept them fully informed because the lack of information only led to rumors and poor morale, and we worked together regardless of whether we were political or career employees. It was all about the mission; if you were on board with it, you were on the team.

The career folks at SBA did a wonderful thing my last week there and threw me a surprise party. Another career civil servant took me aside later and told me that was never done for a political appointee in the past and that I should consider it an honor. I did.

I went to work in the private sector and soon found myself back in the Department of Homeland Security, but this time as a contractor. It was during that time that Steve Cooper, my friend, boss and mentor, resigned as the department's CIO. I learned I was on a short list of potential replacements for Steve and I hoped that God was giving me a second chance. I wasn't picked, however, and the impression I got was that the person who was selected was perceived as less of a troublemaker than me. My background made me better suited for the work, but I wasn't politically correct.

I reached a critical decision at that time: I was tired of trying to make a difference while subordinating myself to someone else's agenda. I decided that someday I was going to be the one setting the agenda. I didn't know how it was going to happen and I still had a job to do for my company and my family.

Mike Brown and I had lunch shortly after he returned from an overseas trip with Florida governor Jeb Bush and Secretary of State Colin Powell to the countries struck by the deadly tsunami in 2004. He said the experience moved him deeply and he came back unwilling to play the Washington game anymore. He indicated he was going to step down soon and I thought his departure from FEMA was imminent. Regrettably for him, he was still in place when Hurricane Katrina hit and he became the scapegoat for everything that went wrong in the response and recovery effort.

When he announced his resignation, I wondered how much different his life would have been if he had resigned shortly after we'd had lunch. FEMA had earned much goodwill from the state of Florida for its response to four hurricanes in one season making landfall on the peninsula. He would have ridden off into the sunset with his head held high and his name unspoiled. As it turned out, I'm sure he, like me, had some pretty candid conversations with God about why it had to go down like it did.

As for my decision to define my own political path, I figured I'd start by becoming involved with my local Republican Party. Before attending the first meeting, I introduced myself via email to the chairman of the local GOP and sent her a copy of my bio.

When I walked into the meeting, every member of the Calvert County Republican Central Committee sitting at the table had a copy of my bio in his or her hands. By the time the meeting had concluded, they had persuaded me to consider running for office.

It was all very sudden and I was overwhelmed by the thought. The election was less than 10 months away and I had no campaign infrastructure and a full-time job. As the expectations rose, I was sitting in my basement office one day, pondering whether or not I should do it. Suddenly, the thought popped into my head, "If not now, when?"

Eerily, my best friend told me days later that he and his wife were talking about my situation and she said to him, "If not now, when?" That pushed me into the deep end of the pool. In February 2006, I announced my candidacy for the U.S. Congress, running against then-House Minority Whip Steny Hoyer.

My campaign drew the attention of the Maryland Republican Party and, when I was summoned to meet with state party officials in late June, I thought it was so they could endorse my campaign or offer their assistance.

Much to my surprise, they asked if I could switch races and run instead against Maryland state Senator Thomas V. "Mike" Miller, a state legislator since 1971, and president of the Maryland Senate since 1987. I even received a call from Governor Bob Ehrlich, Maryland's first Republican governor in over 40 years, encouraging me to make the switch. After a few days of anguished discussion and prayer, I agreed.

Some people labeled me opportunistic or indecisive. My explanation didn't seem to placate them, yet had I continued with my race for Congress, I wouldn't have received any help from the state GOP and I needed them in my corner to win. I was damned if I did and damned if I didn't.

Things went downhill from there—a shorter campaign cycle, retooling our messaging and internet presence for the new opponent, staffing changes—everything swamped us. When the promised "help" arrived from the state GOP, it consisted of a young hire whose job it was to tell me what to do and report back to the headquarters on my progress.

Election Day 2006 started out sunny and I worked a polling place with one of Mike Miller's key lieutenants. We spent the time getting acquainted and passing out campaign literature. By the time I was ready to move on to another polling place, she thanked me for the company and told me I wasn't at all what she thought I'd be. I found her comment amusing and sad at the same time. I wondered what kind of caricature she'd formed in her mind about me without ever having met me.

By the time I'd reached the next polling station, it was raining and we were in the middle of a major controversy that scuttled any chance I might have had, if I had any at all, of winning the election.

I wasn't the only black Republican on the ballot. Maryland Lt. Gov. Michael Steele was in a competitive race against Rep. Ben Cardin for the U.S. Senate seat to be vacated by retiring Sen. Paul Sarbanes.

A Prince George's County political operative had persuaded the Ehrlich and Steele campaigns to pay a group of homeless people from Philadelphia to come down to Prince George's County, and pass out a flyer at the polls with a sample ballot for voters to bring in with them.

The flyer had photos of three prominent black Maryland Democrats on the front with the heading "Ehrlich-Steele Democrats." They were former Congressman Kweisi Mfume, former Prince George's County Executive Wayne Curry, and Jack Johnson, the incumbent county executive.

The inside of the flyer said, "These are our choices" and it listed a mix of Republicans and Democrats that supposedly had garnered the endorsement of the three men pictured on the front.

I first saw the flyer when a white van pulled up to the first polling place I worked. The driver dumped the homeless men and a box of flyers for them to pass out. I grabbed one of the flyers and felt my anger rising as I read it. Not only was I unaware of this flyer and listed in it without my knowledge or permission, but I knew it to be a lie.

None of the men pictured on the flyer had endorsed Governor Ehrlich and only Wayne Curry had endorsed Michael Steele for U.S. Senate. Certainly, I'd not received a formal endorsement from any of them, nor had I requested one.

I ordered the homeless men to take a seat and confiscated their flyers. It was a futile gesture because similar drop-offs had occurred all over Prince George's County, and the flyer had been mailed out to thousands of homes the night before.

At the second polling station I worked that day, I witnessed people standing in line at the polls with this flyer clutched in their fists, and they left no doubt of their intentions once they were inside. I tried to pass out some of my literature and, in many cases, it was politely but firmly rejected. I heard through the grapevine that Representatives Cardin and Hoyer were on TV flogging the state GOP in general and the Ehrlich and Steele campaigns in particular, for their attempts at deception. County Executive Jack Johnson also criticized those responsible for the flyer.

I was convinced that every person with an "R" after his name on the ballot was going to pay dearly for this poorly thought out decision and I was crestfallen because I was innocent of any wrongdoing in this instance.

I heard from another source that someone had posted a bunch of signs on the roads near FedEx Field, sporting the colors of the Black Power flag—red, black and green—and declaring, "I will not be a slave to the Democrats." Those same colors were featured on the deceptive flyer. This was clearly an orchestrated effort to stir black emotions and invoke black pride as a reason to vote Republican and, as it turned out, it was the brainchild of a black Democrat on the Ehrlich payroll.

In retrospect, I'm not surprised. Emotional appeals to black pride and anger aren't the GOP's style and they tend to prefer coalition-building free from racial tension.

As the day wound down, I remember looking up into the rainy sky and whispering to God, "Please give me the strength to bear this." The polls hadn't even closed, but I knew I had lost.

I went to the Huntingtown Volunteer Fire Department to watch the election returns with my family and friends. My mother had flown up from Lake Charles to be with us for the campaign's home stretch and I'm sure God brought her there to comfort me.

One of the more gut wrenching memories from that evening was reading the handwritten name tag that my son, Colin, was wearing. Just below his name, he had written, "Ron Miller's Son." His pride in me was almost more than I could bear.

I also remember how touched my mother was by the genuine love and affection my supporters, most of them white, had for me. Whatever racial tension there was out there in that dark, rainy night, it didn't follow me into that room.

The initial returns were in my favor and they stayed that way long enough for me to hope that maybe my premonition about losing was wrong. Sadly, as the evening wore on it was clear that, despite the assurances from the state GOP that the voters in the district were looking for a viable alternative to Mike Miller, I was going to be defeated soundly. As it turned out, I was one of many Republican casualties in the nationwide tsunami that brought the Democrats to power in Washington and solidified the 150-year plus one-party monopoly in Annapolis.

As I drove my family home, Colin was sitting in the front seat, struggling to hold back his tears. I could feel my heart breaking as I watched him and, once we pulled into the parking lot, he leapt out of the car and raced to his room.

I went into the basement, claiming I was going to watch the rest of the returns. That was partially true. Mostly, I wanted to be alone with my emotions. My mother came down with me and was determined to sit with me until she felt sure I was okay. I finally encouraged her to go to bed and get some rest. I thanked her for being there for me. As soon as I was certain she was no longer in earshot, I broke down and sobbed uncontrollably.

"God, if this was Your will, then why did You let this happen?" I wailed. I was so sure I was following God's path for me, so certain I was going to pull off the upset, that I drove our family into debt to pay campaign expenses and make up for the income we lost when I took a six-week leave of absence from work. My finances were a shambles, I was publicly humiliated by the loss and my son, who proudly declared himself as belonging to me, was shattered by his dad's defeat.

Amid my raw, unfiltered scream of pain toward God, I *heard* a voice. I didn't hear it as if it were spoken, but it sort of landed in my brain. "Do you trust Me?" someone asked. I paused. Then I either thought or said, "Yes." I just don't remember which. I knew then I had no right to be mad at God, because He doesn't make mistakes. I did and they burden me to this day, but I had no right to question His sovereignty. Thus, I recall Job's humility:

> *Then Job answered the LORD and said, "I know that You can do all things, and that no purpose of Yours can be thwarted. 'Who is this that hides counsel without knowledge?' Therefore I have declared that which I did not understand, things too wonderful for me, which I did not know. 'Hear, now, and I will speak; I will ask You, and You instruct me.' I have heard of You by the hearing of the ear; but now my eye sees You; Therefore I retract, and I repent in dust and ashes."*[t]

I'd like to say that from that moment on, my family and I began to heal and move forward. Truth be told, it's been hard. I've been laid off three times in three years, which has to be some kind of record. During that time, I also suffered a serious bout of depression, and I had

---

[t] Job 42:1-6.

to abort my 2010 run for political office after the third layoff.

I still believe in a purposeful God and I try to look at these trials not for the pain they bring, but for the lessons they offer or the strengthening they bring. He's preparing me for something great. I don't know what it is, but it will come according to His timing and to His glory. As Pastor Rich Warren of Saddleback Community Church says in his book, *The Purpose-Driven Life*, "It's not about you."

That said, again I turn to Job: "The LORD gave and the LORD has taken away. Blessed be the name of the LORD."[u]

---

[u] Job 1:21.

-10-

Authentically Black

*"I ain't that black," said Colin Powell
when asked what accounted for his success
and renown in a predominantly white society.*

O ne of the more amusing things about white liberal
Democrats is that, every now and then, their true
feelings about black people will slip out and the resulting
firestorm has them stumbling all over themselves to not
only apologize, but also to tell blacks all the great things
they've done to advance their civil rights.

Yeah, those things have worked so well that we have
a permanent underclass of black people without strong
families, without quality education, without jobs and
without hope. But I digress.

The book *Game Change*, a salacious account of the
2008 presidential campaign written by journalists John
Heilemann and Mark Halperin, recounts how Senate
Majority Leader Harry Reid of Nevada was exulting
over the possibility that one of his new charges, Barack
Obama, the junior senator from Illinois, would run for
president.

He was genuinely impressed by Sen. Obama's cha-
risma and oratorical skills. Reid thought Obama had
a legitimate shot at becoming the nation's first black
president—especially since, as Reid said privately, he
is a "light-skinned" black man "with no Negro dialect,
unless he wanted to have one." Oops.

When these revelations became public in advance of the book's release, Reid was quick to issue a public apology and called President Obama to apologize to him directly. President Obama called the statement "unfortunate," but accepted his apology and declared the matter "closed." Other Democrats, black members of Congress and self-anointed black leaders like the Rev. Al Sharpton also rallied around Reid.

Annoyed Republicans, remembering how former Senate Majority Leader Trent Lott of Mississippi was hounded out of his position in 2002 for comments deemed racially insensitive, decried the double standard. They also suggested, quite correctly in my view, that if Reid's words had been attributed to Senate Minority Leader Mitch McConnell, a Republican, their reaction would have been predictably shrill and harsh. McConnell would have been draped in Klan robes and ridden out of town.

It's not the first time President Obama has been the subject of awkward comments from condescending white liberals about his public appeal. Early in the 2008 presidential race, then-Sen. Joseph Biden of Delaware caused a minor tempest when he offered his assessment of then-candidate Obama's popularity:

I mean, you got the first mainstream African-American who is articulate and bright and clean and a nice-looking guy. I mean, that's a storybook, man.

While Sen. Obama himself didn't take offense, many blacks did because it implied they were not "articulate and bright and clean." While they fixated on the "clean" part (Biden said it was an expression his mother used that meant "clean as a whistle," rather than a hygienic reference), they glossed over or denied the kernel of truth in his use of the word "articulate." Many blacks equate speaking proper English with "talking white." This suggests even they perceive an observable distinction between typical black speech patterns and blacks whose speech is more mainstream in its orientation.

I remember arguing on local message boards with other blacks who genuinely took offense at whites referring to well-spoken blacks as articulate. The offended parties fell into one of two categories: they were offended either because of the underlying assumption in that statement that most blacks are inarticulate or incapable of speaking proper English, or they were offended because they believed being articulate isn't confined to "talking white."

It's insincere of anyone to profess indignation at the implication that blacks don't speak what linguists formally refer to as "Standard American English." There's a commonly accepted archetype of the "authentic black"— blacks know it and whites do too. It's the same archetype that led my grandfather to declare my brother, who has struggled with addictions for most of his life, "black through and through" while I was a "white cake with chocolate frosting."

Colin Powell put it honestly and quite bluntly. He was the "Great Black Hope" for president long before Obama came along and when he was asked in 1995 to explain his universal appeal, even to white people, he said "I speak reasonably well, like a white person" and, visually, "I ain't that black."

The "authentic black" archetype is a person descended from West Africans brought forcibly to America as slaves—African and Caribbean immigrants who came of their own volition need not apply. The "authentic black" is dark-skinned with distinctive "black" features, urban, poor or working class at best in economic status and liberal in political ideology. Culturally, the archetype includes a preference for certain types of fashion, food and music.

The archetype was used satirically by black author Toni Morrison when she referred to President Bill Clinton as "our first Black president," saying that "Clinton displays almost every trope of blackness: single-parent household, born poor, working-class, saxophone-playing, McDonald's-and-junk-food-loving boy from Arkansas."

Incidentally, Clinton had his "first black president" title revoked during the 2008 presidential race because he made veiled racially charged comments to bolster the candidacy of his wife, then-Sen. Hillary Rodham Clinton, and marginalize Sen. Obama as a black candidate who couldn't appeal to the majority of the electorate. In *Game Change*, the authors recount the late Sen. Ted Kennedy's anger with Clinton's attempts to win his support for Hillary. Reportedly, Clinton had belittled Obama in the process, at one point telling Kennedy, "A few years ago, this guy would have been getting us coffee."

Another aspect of President Clinton's circumstances that led to Morrison's satirical label was his "persecution" by "the man" (in his case, the Republicans) over his numerous extramarital affairs, among other transgressions. Clinton's sexual promiscuity hinted at an embellishment of the "authentic black" archetype by some to incorporate passion and physicality, expressed in athletic prowess, dancing, singing skills and sexual performance.

These embellishments of the archetype are embraced by many blacks with pride because of our accomplishments in sports and entertainment, so there's the implication that we are superior lovers too.

These inferences, however, are primarily detritus from the old South, whose white denizens sought to portray black men as bestial and black women as oversexed, both ruled more by their appetites than intelligence, reason or common sense. In that context, they are much less flattering.

Perhaps the most enduring component of the archetype deals with speech. Linguists have labeled it "African

American Vernacular English (AAVE)," "Black English," "Black Vernacular," "Black English Vernacular (BEV)," or "Black Vernacular English (BVE)." The popular term is "Ebonics," derived from "ebony + phonetics."

When a black person is called "articulate," it usually means he or she stands out from the archetype by speaking Standard American English rather than AAVE, BEV or whatever term one chooses to use.

The first time I recall the word "articulate" being used to describe my speaking style was during my senior year in high school in Abilene, Texas. My mother, brother and I were out shopping for shoes for my brother. While they were evaluating different pairs of shoes and the salesman stood by patiently, I must have offered some kind of advice because the salesman turned to my mother and complimented me for being an "articulate" young man.

I don't recall being indignant about it. In fact, I was rather pleased. Every time I traveled home to Lake Charles, my speaking style was always an object of curiosity, jokes or mean-spirited comments from strangers and relatives alike. I was happy to have someone acknowledge that "talkin' propah" was commendable.

Was the salesman deliberately insulting? Absolutely not. He was paying me and my mother a compliment, so we graciously accepted it as such. After all, being called "articulate" in Abilene wasn't a racially motivated statement. In a city where most people spoke with a West Texas drawl, anyone who spoke with precise diction and no discernable accent would stand out, regardless of skin color!

I knew that speaking was one of the gifts God had given me. My favorite class in my senior year at Abilene Cooper High School was Mr. Ralph Thornhill's speech class. My communications teacher at Texas Tech chided me for not developing my non-verbal communications skills and trying to get by on my "excellent speaking voice."

Still, I knew one of the reasons I was often complimented for my speaking style was because Standard American English wasn't expected of me. President George W. Bush called that attitude "the soft bigotry of low expectations."

I remember taking someone's order while working a fast food drive-thru and the person complimented me on my voice, saying I should be on radio. I thanked him. When he pulled around to pay for and pick up his order, he saw that I was black and the look on his face was priceless.

Remember my election in college as the first black executive vice chairman of the College Republicans of Texas? I'm convinced it came about due to the novelty I represented, not just because of my conservative political views, but also because of how I spoke.

Until I gave my speech, no one there knew anything about me. I had joined my campus College Republicans chapter just three months earlier. The only things that distinguished me from the other candidates with more "time in grade," as we used to say in the military, were my race and my speaking voice.

After volunteering on George W. Bush's failed bid for the Congress the year before, in 1980 a friend and I started a Texas Tech chapter for his father, who was running for president. I was the primary liaison between our fledgling chapter and the George Bush for President campaign headquarters in Houston. I spent many hours on the phone with one of the campaign operatives to plan a visit by then-Ambassador Bush to the campus.

When this operative finally came up to meet in person with my friend and me, he extended his hand in greeting to my friend, who was white, and proclaimed how great it was to finally meet me. I politely pointed out to him that I, not my friend, was the one with whom he'd been interacting over the phone. He was embarrassed but I was gracious about his mistake and we pressed on with the matters at hand.

My speaking ability had an early impact on my professional life as well. At my first Air Force assignment for air intelligence officer training, my end-of-course evaluation said, "He demonstrated an outstanding oral communication skill and was one of the best briefers in his class."

During my next assignment at Strategic Air Command (SAC) headquarters in Omaha, Nebraska, I served as an analyst and supported the command intelligence briefers with information they needed for their daily presentations to the SAC chief of intelligence and the SAC commander-in-chief. I was commended for being "articulate and eloquent when presenting briefings."

The chief of the SAC intelligence briefing team noted my presence, speaking skills and ability to think on my feet, so he requested that I audition for a spot on the briefing team. Frankly, I didn't want the job because it was one of the more grueling jobs in intelligence and the opportunities to fail spectacularly in front of several generals and other superiors, peers and subordinates were numerous.

Duty called, however, and I auditioned for the position. I thought—and hoped—my chances of being selected were slim. I was only a second lieutenant with barely a year of active military service and the briefing team was staffed with more senior officers. I was auditioning along with two or three other officers, all of whom were senior to me.

Despite the odds, I was selected, making me the youngest briefer on the team in recent memory. While I didn't want the job, I excelled at it and each of my officer evaluation reports from this time frame used the word "articulate" in the "Oral Communication" block to describe my speaking skills.

Since then, I've delivered hundreds of speeches to a variety of audiences ranging from a home group to a convention center with thousands, and I'm accustomed by now to whites using the "A" word to describe my speeches. It's really never bothered me and, frankly, I prefer it to "He talk like a white boy!" The implication that speaking Standard American English is a skill only white people can master is demeaning, whether we realize it or not.

I've been an executive in the armed forces, private industry, the federal government and the headquarters of a national non-profit organization. In reality, Standard American English is the *lingua franca* of successful people in the workplace.

In addition, to summarize the thoughts in a column I read many years ago by writer and author William Raspberry, those who speak with precise diction and good grammar are immediately credited with intelligence, regardless of their true mental acuity. Those who choose to speak black English, or southern redneck or Texas drawl, for that matter, will probably need to produce further evidence of their intellectual achievements before they are extended the same presumption.

Within one's own family, neighborhood or community, a person can speak in whatever language or dialect he or she wishes, but no one should expect that to be accepted outside of those circles. That's not a commentary on race or culture or a repudiation of either. The same rule applies to white southerners or any other ethnic group. Articulate speech is a major contributor to professional success. Leave the dialect at home.

If you lived abroad, you would be compelled to learn the common language of the nation in which you reside in order to survive and eventually thrive. Why should America be any different?

Some blacks get hung up on the word "articulate" because of the implication that black English is somehow "inarticulate." They point to orators like Jesse Jackson, Al Sharpton, Dr. Martin Luther King, Jr. and others as a challenge to the notion that people who speak in the cadences, dialect and inflections of the black community aren't "articulate."

I've no doubt these speakers are "eloquent"—powerful, persuasive and emotionally expressive. Nevertheless, to be articulate, at least in the minds of those using the term, is to be very precise and deliberate with the spoken word, to enunciate one's words.

Oprah Winfrey and Jesse Jackson can be articulate or eloquent, or both, but whites typically associate articulateness with Winfrey because of her precise diction. It's a valuable skill for a broadcaster and cross-cultural television personality. At the height of his influence, Jackson was regarded by many as eloquent because of the power of his speaking to move an audience, a critical talent for a pastor or politician.

One of the great black orators of recent history was Barbara Jordan, a member of the U.S. Congress from Texas who gained notoriety as a result of the Watergate hearings. She had a distinct, larger than life voice that was uniquely hers. I've not heard anything quite like it before or since. One author described her voice as "eloquent thunder" and the term fits.

Her keynote speech to the Democratic National Convention in 1976 was considered by historians to be one of the top 100 American speeches of the 20th century, and the best keynote speech of modern times, until a virtually unknown state legislator named Barack Obama transfixed the Democrats at their 2004 convention.

It is telling to note that, in a culture where black children look askance at one of their own who "talks white," something that's been going on since I was a child in school, two of the finest speeches in American history were delivered by a black woman and a black man.

President Obama is a master communicator because he understands articulateness and eloquence, and employs both as skillfully as anyone I've seen or heard in recent years. He's taken the precision of language gained from his unconventional upbringing and elite education, melded it with the cadences and inflections of the black pastor, and punctuated it will the resonance and richness of his God-given baritone, the most appealing of all the registers when it comes to public speaking. The results, as we've witnessed over the past five years since his keynote speech, are electric.

When I was in college, I was a member of an organization called the Black Republicans of Texas. Many of the founding members were pastors, and I admired their ability to fire up a crowd, even as I lamented the fact my precise, academic manner of speaking seemed to elicit only polite applause.

I was expressing my admiration to one of our leaders one day after watching him move his audience with his words, and I was critical of my own speaking style. He told me, "We always need people who speak like you." I'm not sure I believed him.

Decades later, I find myself listening to Charles Lollar, a black friend and Republican candidate for public office, and marveling at his ability to meld the speaking styles of black pastor, Marine officer and senior business executive into a compelling whole.

I've seen people from all races and political backgrounds brought to their feet when he speaks, and I believe because he communicates in a way that transcends racial and ethnic boundaries, he will be more persuasive than I ever will be in bringing new, non-traditional constituencies to the GOP.

That brings me back to the central question; can a black person speak Standard American English, present a polished, businesslike demeanor, win the praise of whites for his or her poise, and still be authentically black in the eyes of other blacks? I'd like to believe there is room for all manner of styles in the black community, just as there is in other racial and ethnic communities.

I don't know if other ethnic groups struggle like we do with diversity in our own ranks, but our uniqueness as individuals should be a cause for celebration, not condemnation. All our battles for liberty and acceptance as equal heirs to the American Dream are in vain if we aren't free to be whoever God made us to be.

Guess Who's Coming to Dinner

*"I don't care to see a member of my own
race getting above himself...Civil rights
is one thing. This here is somethin' else."*
~ *Isabel Sanford as Tillie in*
Guess Who's Coming to Dinner

As I write this, professional golfer extraordinaire Eldrick Tont "Tiger" Woods is enduring a rough patch in his personal life.

You would think that a man who, at the end of 2009, was named the Professional Golf Association Tour Player of the Year for the 10th time in 13 years, and Athlete of the Decade by the Associated Press, would be dusting off a spot in the trophy case for his latest haul, with his beautiful wife, Elin, and two young children by his side.

Unfortunately for Tiger, it's more likely that the wife and kids are living elsewhere while he sits alone in his Windermere, Florida estate. Given Elin's alacrity with a golf club—obviously, she took well to those golf lessons he gave her!—he might want to place security at his bedroom door in case she stops by to pick up her things.

In the aftermath of an early morning car crash in the driveway with Tiger behind the wheel, the American public learned that the golfer with discipline on the course had not been so disciplined with his libido off the course.

Thus far, depending on what sources you trust, Tiger has been sexually involved with 10-15 women over the past few years, only one of whom was his wife. The revelation of serial infidelity has shattered the image he had so carefully crafted—steely-eyed assassin on the golf course, devoted husband and father off of it, and arguably the most popular athlete in the world.

As Tiger's reputation crumbles, the black community is once again thrust into the position of determining whether another of its prodigal sons is worthy of being reclaimed, a la O.J. Simpson.

They have never been quite sure what to make of Tiger. On the one hand, he doesn't consider himself strictly black and famously coined the phrase "Cablanasian" (Caucasian, black, Native American and Asian) to describe his ethnic makeup. He has preferred to build a public image accessible to the widest possible audience and therefore shunned controversial topics like race, civil rights and the plight of urban America.

As an example, when a female golf commentator and friend jokingly suggested the only way anyone could beat Tiger at golf was to "lynch him in a back alley," the black community was outraged and the comment was all over the internet, talk radio and the news channels. While the commentator was eventually suspended for two weeks, Tiger Woods declared, "It was unfortunate... Kelly and I did speak. There was no ill intent. She regrets saying it. In my eyes, it's all said and done."

This response was inadequate as far as National Football League Hall of Famer Jim Brown was concerned. He said Tiger should have come out sooner and not taken the politically correct route in his statement. Tiger and Brown haven't been the best of friends and, in the following year, Brown criticized Tiger for not being "an individual for social change."

On the other hand, blacks embrace him because of his unmatched excellence in one of the "whitest" of sports. While he wasn't the first black golfer, he is so dominant in the sport that black children can actually envision themselves on the links at the local country club. His Tiger Woods Foundation has helped over 10 million children to reach their goals in life through scholarships, junior golf teams, grants, and learning and character development programs—yes, in hindsight there's some irony in that.

So where do they stand on his infidelity? Not where you'd expect.

It seems the angst in the black community has little to do with his cheating and more to do with his choice of sexual partners. It was unsettling enough to many blacks that he married a so-called Barbie doll from Sweden, but to find out that all the women with whom he was sexually involved were white touched a nerve, especially among black women.

One young black woman commented to the press that "There's just this preservation thing we have among one another. We like to see each other with each other." President Barack Obama's biracial background became less of an issue for him with blacks because he was married to a black woman. The same young woman also said, "Had Barack had a white wife, I would have thought twice about voting for him."

You don't have to be famous to be affected by this attitude, either. As my advisors and I developed a campaign strategy for my second run for elected office, one of the topics of discussion was how the voters in mostly black Prince George's County would react to pictures of me with my family since my wife is white. The consensus among those who live in that county was that it would be negatively received. I love my wife and I'm not ashamed of her, so I had no plans to change anything. Still, the potential public fallout over my 26-year interracial marriage bothered me.

Many white Americans are being exposed to this attitude in the black community toward interracial relationships for the first time and some are incredulous that blacks, of all people, would harbor such racist attitudes. After all, isn't that the kind of thinking that put blacks in chains and denied them their civil rights? What would blacks say if a white person suggested that whites and blacks should date and marry their own kind exclusively?

We actually know the answer to that question. Last year, a Louisiana justice of the peace refused to sign the marriage license of an interracial couple because he didn't believe in "mixed marriages." In his opinion, the children of such marriages would be harmed because they wouldn't be accepted by either race. The public reaction to his actions, which were inappropriate and against the law, was swift and fierce. Eventually he was forced to resign. Civil rights groups were at the front of the line demanding his resignation. So they'll fight for the right of this interracial couple to marry, even as they object to black men marrying outside their race?

In response, most blacks with this mindset would say, "You wouldn't understand." They make a clear distinction between civil rights and matters of culture and love. In other words, blacks cheer the *Loving v. Virginia* Supreme Court decision ending race-based legal restrictions on marriage in America. Famous or well-off black men dating and marrying outside of their race? Not so much.

The reasons I've heard for this tension are many, but here's a sampling of a few popular perceptions:

- Black men, especially the rich and famous, see white women as trophies signifying they've "made it" in society. They are a visual indicator of upward mobility.

- Black men think white women are more docile and compliant than black women, who they view as loud, domineering and disrespectful of their manhood.
- Black men see non-black women, especially white women, as previously "forbidden fruit" ripe for the picking and they are gorging on it.
- Famous or well-to-do black men find it easier to attract women of all races, so they aren't limited in their choices.
- Black men suffer from arrested self-esteem due to generations of emasculation caused by slavery and discrimination, and dating or marrying a white woman helps them to elevate their sense of self.
- Black men are "victims" of cultural indoctrination which has always held up white women, especially blonde white women, as the pinnacle of female beauty.

I may have missed some, but the point should be clear. Equally compelling are the opinions of black women who object to interracial dating and marriage:

- So many black men are poor, uneducated or undereducated, unemployed or underemployed, or in the prison system that black women have fewer choices of mates.
- Many black men are "gangstas" or "gangsta" wannabes, and thus not appealing as partners, further limiting the available pool of mates.
- White men are indoctrinated by the same cultural definition of female beauty as black men, and women of color, especially black women, are generally not attractive to them.
- Black women are the guardians of the black family and feel an obligation to hold it together

against all onslaughts, particularly its dilution by non-blacks.

It is against this backdrop that I'm recounting my journey of discovery with the opposite sex. Just as I was naïve about racism and discrimination growing up, I was equally unaware of the dynamics of race and sex in our society. I was simply practicing what I'd been taught about color being insignificant in human relationships, platonic or otherwise, while others reacted with incredulity and hostility to my presumption.

I remember befriending a pretty blonde in 4th and 5th grade, and we shared an interest in Smokey the Bear and forestry (no, I can't explain it!). We used to plant pine cones thinking we were creating new forests for future generations.

We were a platonic pair but one day she came to me and said we couldn't spend time together anymore because her father disapproved of her being with a black boy. I was disappointed but she immediately introduced me to her friend who was also interested in forestry and could take her place. Although she was also white, I guess her father didn't have any qualms about her hanging out with me or he didn't know. It didn't matter to me. We started planting pine cones together as if nothing was amiss.

During one of our stays in Louisiana while I was in junior high school, I befriended a girl who was a friend of the family. We used to talk for hours about the world and everything in it. I had big dreams and she loved listening to my plans. We were just friends, but she was the kind of girl my grandfather approved of, a black girl with skin and features so fair she could have passed for white.

I was always bemused by my grandfather's stated preference for light-skinned black girls over white or dark-skinned ones, especially since he was as black as black can be. The logic that my dates shouldn't be too white or too black escaped me. If it was his personal preference, there was no reason it should apply to me. I somehow managed to avoid the socialization that leads many to prefer only people of a particular race or skin color. I've been attracted to women who were white as snow, brown as caramel or black as coal. I have no racial litmus test for female beauty.

When we accompanied my dad to Spain, I was in those awkward teenage years where I was both attracted to and afraid of girls. I had a crush on a pretty biracial girl beginning in 8th grade and lasting until the first half of my 11th grade year. We were never more than friends, however. The one time I had an opportunity to take her out on a date, I was literally dragged to her locker, goaded into asking her out and, after she said yes, I avoided her like the plague until she sensed my reluctance and released me from my obligation.

By my junior year in high school, we were in a class together for the first time since 8th grade and through a number of shared class projects, I discovered she had a beautiful and winning personality to complement her outer beauty. Just as we were getting to know each other, it was time for us to move again. I was an idiot.

In fact, I was considered by the girls in school to be the "nice guy," the one who treated them with respect and never leered at them or made crude sexual references toward them. I never quite understood why guys thought such boorish behavior was attractive to a girl, but it gave me an advantage in that I had a number of female friends who liked and trusted me.

One of them cried when she heard I was leaving because I had been so kind to her. I defended her honor when some of my baseball teammates were lying about her, accusing her of the most horrible things, simply because she wouldn't go out with any of them.

Another of my friends, a petite white girl, was my permanent dance partner at all the school dances. We'd meet at the dance and spend the entire evening together, then go our separate ways until the next dance. We never went out otherwise and there were no expectations other than the promise of good company at the dances. She felt safe and relaxed around me and I was honored that she found comfort in my presence.

One girl that made me very uncomfortable, however, was an assertive black girl who wore too much makeup and dressed too provocatively for school. We weren't friends, but she seemed to take pleasure in embarrassing me with her occasional come-ons. Once she blocked my path to the library, where I usually went after lunch to read before the next class period. I had "nerd" stamped on my forehead, making me an inviting target for teasing, and she flirted with me until I begged her to let me pass. She pulled the same stunt in high school, putting herself between me and my destination, with her male friends blocking my exit to the rear. That time, she stole a kiss before she let me pass. I was humiliated.

Since all of these adventures occurred on a military base, we were attending integrated schools and living in integrated housing. Interracial dating wasn't unusual, especially among the high school students, and I had no inkling of the issues surrounding black-white relationships. I also believe that being stationed in a foreign country caused us to bond together as Americans and we didn't have time for a lot of drama over racial differences.

Abilene, Texas was another matter. As I mentioned before, my father's assignment to Abilene was the first time we'd lived at a military installation where I went to school off-base. Kids from military families mingled with the locals at Abilene Cooper High School. I arrived at the half-year point of my junior year, so I didn't know a lot of people by the time summer arrived.

Between my junior and senior year, I worked at a summer camp for people with disabilities and was attracted to a perky, pretty brunette who was a student counselor like me. We had a brief fling that consisted of a single kiss and some hand holding, but at the farewell party she quashed any notions of us having a relationship beyond summer camp.

I was a rather sensitive and emotional young man. Because she was my first kiss, I took her rejection pretty hard. I knew I'd see her again because we went to the same school and lived in base housing. Little did I know the can of worms my infatuation with her was about to open.

Her father was an officer at the same air base where we lived, so I presumed that a man with a college degree and an officer's commission was educated, enlightened and had no issues with race.

When I paid her a surprise visit at her house one evening, I was quickly ushered outside the house by her father, who asked me to please notify them in the future if I wanted to come over so they could be "prepared." "Prepared for what?" I wondered, but I knew what he meant.

The girl's mother went to the local grocery store where my mother worked and told her that I needed to learn my place or words to that effect. One of the first and worst arguments I ever had with my mother was over this girl and my infatuation with her. I must have said something disrespectful to her because she slapped me. That's the only time I can remember her doing that to me and it hurt worse inside than outside.

I was so messed up over this girl that I literally made myself sick and missed a month of school.

That wasn't the only episode I experienced in my senior year involving a white girl. Just before the senior prom, a friend of mine broke up with his girlfriend, an attractive blonde who any guy would have been thrilled to date. Desperate to show her ex-boyfriend that she could have a good time without him, she asked if I would take her to the prom. Surprised but excited, I said yes. I rented a black tux and patent leather shoes, which were too tight. I did everything I could to prepare for a special night with one of the prettiest girls in school on my arm.

Except it didn't quite work out that way. My male friend who drove us to the prom ordered me to stay in the car while he went to retrieve my date from her house. He had said something about her father being a cop. I thought, "Okay, this isn't starting off really well."

Once we got to the prom, my date had no problem dancing with me during the fast songs but wouldn't slow dance with me. At some point, I remember sitting down because my feet hurt and looking onto the dance floor, only to see my date slow-dancing with another boy I didn't know—a white boy. I knew then what was going on.

I sat there with a frozen grin on my face and a cup of punch. When my friend came over and asked me if I was okay, I said, "Can we go home?" We left my date with whatever guy she'd picked up and my friend took me home. What was supposed to be a night to remember ended up being just that, but not in the way I'd imagined.

The girl did come to me days later in tears to apologize, saying she didn't intend to hurt my feelings. Of course I accepted her apology—I always did because my faith and my upbringing taught me that forgiveness was among the highest of virtues. Besides, it wasn't like she and I were in a steady relationship. She was using me to make her ex jealous and I allowed her to do it. I probably shouldn't have expected much out of the evening given the circumstances.

I write about the conflicts that arose from my relationships with white girls, but I don't want to leave the impression that I had a particular bias or preference toward one race when it came to women. In college, I would say I was an equal opportunity dater—that is, when I could get a date. I was pretty shy and, shall we say, "inexperienced" when it came to women, so I was a very late bloomer in that regard.

When I attended summer classes in 1978 at what is now Texas A&M-Kingsville, I had a secret crush on a young lady with whom I performed in the school theater program. To stay in shape, we would go running together and I got to know her as a smart, sweet woman who also happened to be drop-dead beautiful.

Alas, she had a boyfriend. He was a law student and they adored each other. She was a Latina, but I would never know if my being black would have been a problem for her or her family and friends.

The first woman I dated seriously was black and I thought we would get married someday. That's probably what eventually scared her and others off. For me, dating wasn't a sport, it was the pursuit of a marriage partner.

My sporadic and largely unsuccessful dating life in college was a virtual rainbow of races and cultures. I remember one young lady, shy and sweet and black as midnight, who I took out on a date. She was wide-eyed and gorgeous, but she only wanted to hear me talk. I know some of you "fellas" out there are saying, "What's wrong with that?" Well, I enjoy interesting conversation, and a one-sided discussion isn't conversation.

Another woman I went out with was essentially a blind date. She had seen my picture in the school yearbook and called me out of the blue to ask me out. Inexplicably, I agreed to meet her and, as it turned out, she wasn't a stalker or a psychopath. She was raised in a family with a lot of boys and learned to go after what she wanted. She was multiracial, black and Latino, and let's just say that she wore the combination very well.

We found out after our first date, however, that we had nothing in common. We didn't share the same tastes in music and entertainment, and she had little or no interest in current affairs—she didn't even "get" the movie we went to see. We ended up shaking hands and never saw each other again.

Before meeting the woman that would eventually become my wife, the most serious relationship I had in college was with a white graduate student who lived in the same private dorm as I did. She was in her first year of graduate school and I was a sophomore, but we befriended each other and she treated me as if I were mature beyond my years.

She chose me over several of her male peers and classmates to take her to our homecoming festivities one year and, as I recall, that didn't sit well with at least one of them. I, on the other hand, was thrilled. I was still getting over my failed relationship with the girl I thought I would marry someday, so it built up my self-esteem to have my new friend choose me as her date.

We made a full day of it. While I seem to recall her sister and possibly her sister's date joining us, my recollection is fuzzy because I was totally focused on her. I bought her a beautiful corsage to wear to the homecoming game, where we cheered the Texas Tech Red Raiders on to victory.

Afterwards, we had dinner at the only French restaurant in Lubbock. Then we went to see a movie. We finished the evening at a club atop one of the highest buildings in Lubbock, where we danced and looked out over the city while talking about many things. It was a storybook day and I've never forgotten it.

We continued to date and she took a keen interest in my political activities. I invited her to be my guest at a fundraising luncheon for then-Ambassador George H.W. Bush, and we often talked about economics and political philosophy. It was an unusual relationship because we never officially declared it a relationship.

We simply spent time together and enjoyed each other's company.

When I took her to the Air Force ROTC dining-out, a formal affair in military circles, I felt I was the luckiest man in the room. She was elegance and class all the way, and I was honored by her friendship.

When she came one day to tell me she'd become involved with another graduate student, I wished her well. When we had first met, she was recovering from her fiancé of three years dumping her before she left for graduate school, and this new boyfriend seemed to make her happy.

She must have known I was growing fond of her because she took the time to tell me about her relationship, almost as if she were seeking my blessing. She didn't owe me an explanation. I hadn't made a commitment to her nor had she made a commitment to me. We had become the closest of friends, so it meant a lot that she'd come to share the bittersweet news. In other words, I was truly happy for her, but sad because we wouldn't be seeing each other anymore.

Eventually, she broke up with her new boyfriend, but we both ended up meeting our future spouses not long thereafter. After earning her graduate degree, my female friend left Lubbock for her first job, where she fell in love with a coworker.

I met Annik, a lovely French linguistics student who was attending Texas Tech on a semester abroad.

During one of her trips to Lubbock with her fiancé, my friend looked me up and invited me to dinner with them. At dinner, she honored me greatly. Actually, I was worried that her effusive praise would make her husband-to-be jealous!

Our relationship was and remains special for many reasons, not the least of which was the love and respect she showed me as a man rather than a black man. I can't remember my race ever being discussed, not even in casual conversation.

That was also the beauty of my relationship and eventual romance with Annik, who became my wife. Since she wasn't from America, Annik had no preconceived notions about black-white relations. Actually, it was the classic movie about an interracial relationship that sparked our first conversation about race in general and interracial relationships in particular.

A friend had invited several of us to his home to see *Guess Who's Coming to Dinner*. Afterwards, my future bride wondered what the fuss in the movie was all about. I was charmed by her naiveté and proceeded to pontificate on the history of race in America as if I were an expert.

I later learned from her that when she returned to France and announced to her parents we were dating, they were initially worried, but not because I was black. The only dark-skinned people to whom they were regularly exposed were Muslims from northern Africa, and they had seen many young French women marry Muslim men and become subservient to them in accordance with Islamic custom, including Sharia law. Once they discovered I was thoroughly Christian and Western, I was welcomed warmly into the family.

We've been married for 26 years now and we have three amazing children. My reason for marrying her was straightforward and it wasn't on the list I presented previously. Quite simply, I loved her and wanted to spend the rest of my life with her. Her race or country of origin had no bearing on my decision whatsoever.

A romantic relationship shouldn't be about making a social statement or validating oneself in the eyes of society. If it's about anything other than whether or not two people are compatible with each other, the relationship is built on a weak foundation and doomed to failure. By shutting ourselves off from potential partners because of race, we, not anyone else, are cheating our-selves and reducing our options.

There's a big world of possible partners out there whose company is to be enjoyed. Just don't "be a Tiger" and sink your putts all over the place for birdies when you've scored an eagle at home.

-12-

Of God and Caesar

But Peter and the apostles answered,
"We must obey God rather than men."
~ The Acts of the Apostles, 5:29

One fall evening in 2008, while looking for a place to sit in preparation for our church's biannual congregational meeting, a friend yelled at me from across the room to come over to where she was. Once I was within conversational range, she pointed to a fellow church member and said to me, "You need to set her straight!"

It was said half in jest. Both women were in ministry together at the church and were very close. Yet the emphatic nature of my friend's statement made me wonder what the other woman's transgression could be.

A quick glance gave me my answer. My friend's friend was wearing a T-shirt promoting Barack Obama for president. Since most of the people in the church were well aware of my political activism, I guess my friend felt that imbued me with some kind of authority to correct this woman's "error." Not looking to engage in a political debate inside our sanctuary, I made some harmless quip and quickly slipped away.

A lot of Christians and churchgoing people were swayed by Obama in the last election. Well before he announced his run for the presidency, Obama declared that the Democratic Party's hostility toward people of faith had to end if they ever expected to regain political power. He was the first Democratic candidate since Jimmy Carter to make so strong an appeal to the faithful of American society.

He managed to persuade quite a few evangelical Christians and some prominent pro-life advocates that he was a different kind of Democrat who would listen to them and bring their concerns to the table in the hope of finding that ever-so-elusive "common ground."

He declared to the faithful that he was a Christian and he spoke eloquently in an interview with *Newsweek* magazine of his coming to Christ:

> *At the point of his decision to accept Christ, Obama says, "what was intellectual and what was emotional joined, and the belief in the redemptive power of Jesus Christ, that he died for our sins, that through him we could achieve eternal life... I found that powerful."*[21]

Add to that the photo ops of him speaking from the pulpits of various churches, and many Christians practically swooned at his words, believing he was the one who would finally bring an end to the culture wars which had been raging in American society since the early 1980s.

Apparently, far too many Christians were tired of the fight and tired of the world's hostility toward them. They had lost sight of St. Paul's admonition to believers: "Let us not lose heart in doing good, for in due time we will reap if we do not grow weary."[v] They were looking for a way out while still declaring full devotion to Christ and His teachings, and Obama offered them an escape route, or so it appeared.

President Obama clearly understands the power of faith in people's lives and sometimes he speaks the

---

[v] Galatians 6:9.

language of faith with great ease. Many Christians hoped he would be the bridge between the Democrats and the evangelical community, especially the younger evangelicals who espouse a social agenda that includes so-called 'social justice' issues including the environment, poverty, disease, and genocide, along with the traditional hot-button issues of sanctity of life and the protection of traditional marriage.

Yet many of us were skeptical of his claims, particularly since his political track record didn't reflect the influence of Christian values in his life. He was one of the most ardent pro-abortion senators in the Illinois legislature, and he used the phrase "pre-viable fetus" to dehumanize the unborn child and justify his votes against a partial-birth abortion ban.

Let's be clear about what this practice is. An abortionist pulls a late-term baby almost all the way out of his mother's womb, turns the child face down, then stabs him and vacuums out his brain. Even Sen. Daniel Patrick Moynihan, a Democrat, described it as "too close to infanticide." In fact, it is infanticide, but that didn't seem to trouble Obama's conscience.

Obama's comments in a 2004 interview with the *Chicago Sun-Times* led me to doubt the extent of his faith. When asked about his religious beliefs, he said the following:

> *"I am a Christian... I'm rooted in the Christian tradition. I believe that there are many paths to the same place, and that is a belief that there is a higher power, a belief that we are connected as a people."*

Hmm. Jesus declared, "I am the way, and the truth, and the life; no one comes to the Father but through Me."[w] Yet according to Obama, Jesus *really* meant "I am

---

[w] John 14:6.

one of the ways, one of many truths and one of many paths to life. Everyone comes to the Father and some through Me."

When asked who Jesus was to him, Obama responded:

"Jesus is an historical figure for me, and he's also a bridge between God and man, in the Christian faith, and one that I think is powerful precisely because he serves as that means of us reaching something higher.

"And he's also a wonderful teacher. I think it's important for all of us, of whatever faith, to have teachers in the flesh and also teachers in history."

I don't know if President Obama believes that Jesus was fully man and fully God. None of his statements that I've seen suggest that Christ is anything more to him that "an historical figure" and "a wonderful teacher." In that sense, Obama sounds like a lot of people today who refuse to embrace Jesus' divinity, even as they praise His wisdom and character.

Such folks never explain how a man they believe to be wise and good could also declare Himself the Son of God and predict His own death and miraculous resurrection from the grave three days later to fulfill His Father's plan for humankind. A man speaking in this manner today would be considered mentally ill, even if he had moments of great insight and depth.

Only with Christ do we perform the mental gymnastics that allow us to declare Him a great philosopher and teacher, while conveniently ignoring the credible claims He made about who He was and what He had come to earth to do.

President Obama acknowledges Christ's resurrection in some of his public statements, but the awesome heavenly power of that world-changing event has no effect on his rationalization that "all God's children go to heaven" regardless of whether or not they accept Christ as their Lord and Savior.

As Timothy Keller said in his book, *The Reason for God: Belief in an Age of Skepticism*:

> *Sometimes people approach me and say, "I really struggle with this aspect of Christian teaching. I like this part of Christian belief, but I don't think I can accept that part." I usually respond: "If Jesus rose from the dead, then you have to accept all he said; if he didn't rise from the dead, then why worry about any of what he said? The issue on which everything hangs is not whether or not you like his teaching but whether or not he rose from the dead... If Jesus rose from the dead, it changes everything."*

President Obama may speak our language, but he's cut from the same cloth as most liberals because he refuses to acknowledge the Bible in its entirety. During a 2006 speech, he spoke in a mocking tone about the Bible as if it was in error in some areas and not in others:

> *Which passages of Scripture should guide our public policy? Should we go with Leviticus, which suggests slavery is OK and that eating shellfish is abomination? How about Deuteronomy, which suggests stoning your child if he strays from the faith? Or should we just stick to the Sermon on the Mount—a passage that is so radical that it's doubtful that our own Defense Department would survive its application? So before we get carried away, let's read our Bibles. Folks haven't been reading their Bibles.*

Well, I've read and reflected on the Bible for most of my life and Obama clearly doesn't understand the difference between the ceremonial and civil laws of the old covenant, and the moral law which was revealed to us in the Ten Commandments and fulfilled in Jesus Christ and His church.

The Bible is not only a guidebook for holy living, it is also the history of a people, and we would no more adopt the entirety of ancient Jewish customs than we would the practices of early American colonists. The ceremonial and civil laws in the Old Testament were clearly God's instruction and admonition to establish a holy nation in the midst of a pagan land. Those who mock the ceremonial and civil laws to justify ignoring the moral law that is universal and consistent throughout the Word are deceiving themselves and others.

President Obama may be reading his Bible, but his understanding is a work in progress, and he needs to study it further, as all Christians should. It is the daily and in-depth study rather than just the reading of the Bible that teaches us to understand and receive God's Word as He intended it.

President Obama also adopts the liberal position that assumes Jesus' commands to individual Christians and the church are actually calls for government to act as our provider.

Christians fall into the trap of thinking that by promoting the funding of government aid programs, they are doing the Lord's work. The only miracle of Jesus that appears in all four Gospels is the feeding of the 5,000, and I've always been struck by what He told the disciples when they suggested that He send the crowd away to buy food in the nearby villages: "You give them something to eat!"[x]

His words were a *personal* and immediate call to action. Christ didn't tell them to go petition the king for a food aid program, nor did He lead a march against

---

[x] Matthew 14:16; Mark 6:37, Luke 9:13.

poverty down the streets of Jerusalem. He commands us to personally serve our brothers and sisters, rather than using government bureaucracy as a surrogate.

The Acts of the Apostles is often cited by liberals as evidence of Christianity endorsing government action to provide for the less fortunate:

> *And all those who had believed were together and had all things in common; and they began selling their property and possessions and were sharing them with all, as anyone might have need.*[y]

To interpret this passage as a divine directive for redistributive government is either naïve or self-serving. These were the voluntary acts of a church community serving one another, not a compulsory government welfare program. These acts of community and the meeting of needs by family, friends and neighbors are characteristic of a faith that expects its followers to touch people's lives directly. Such intimacy not only meets a person's physical needs, but also helps him to heal.

Jay W. Richards, author of *Money, Greed and God*, illustrates the fallacy of a central government serving as a charity:

> *Replacing a family or a neighborhood or a local church with a federal program for helping the down-and-out is like trying to have an official in the Department of Commerce guess how much I should pay, right now, for a new pair of size-9 Asics running shoes. At the moment, I wouldn't pay much, since I just bought a pair. And I'm picky when it comes to colors. That, and I don't wear size 9! The official could look up the market price for Asics shoes in the United States... That's crucial*

---

[y] Acts 2:44-45.

information. He probably wouldn't know much else, though, so he'd have to guess, and he'd probably guess wrong, and waste his time and mine in the process. That's the information gap in a nutshell. It's impossible to fix a problem if you don't know squat about it.

The principle of subsidiarity, as articulated in Catholic social doctrine, is partially reflected in our Constitution's Tenth Amendment. It teaches that matters should be handled by the person or group closest to the problem because it's at that level where we have the most detailed knowledge and the most responsibility.

It begins with individual responsibility or the family if it's a child or someone unable to take care of themselves. It graduates to the neighbors, then to the local church or non-profit group, after that the local or state government, and then, only as the last resort, the federal government. The farther away the jurisdiction from the specific person or problem, the more general the solution because the knowledge is not as specific. It's not that the federal civil servant is heartless; rather, they're just too far away.

The imposition of the federal government, in Richards' words, "runs roughshod over this intricate web of overlapping responsibilities and assumes knowledge where none exists."

Community aid is not only more efficient and effective, it's personal. When you are looking into the eyes of a father who has lost his job and feels the shame of not being able to provide for his family, and you are offering him not only food but compassion, the value of that kind of human interaction is incalculable.

In the aftermath of Hurricane Katrina, the worst natural disaster in U.S. history, government officials from the local to the federal level were embroiled in hearings, political posturing, name-calling and finger-pointing.

But individuals from private charities and private companies were hard at work restoring the Gulf Coast region, especially in New Orleans.

In particular, faith-based charities made long-term commitments to the wellness of the city. Even churches in my county, including my own, sent people to New Orleans on multiple missions of mercy and love in the months following the disaster, helping to rebuild homes, churches and schools. Church groups provided food, shelter, clothing and medical attention.

Evelyn Turner, a New Orleans resident who lost her home in the flood, found herself in a rebuilt home in her old neighborhood, a blessing made possible by faith-based charities. "The church poured into the city," she said. "Here it is two years later, and who's still coming? The church."[22]

Local aid organizations won't forget you, lose your file or treat you like a number. You're not just a case to them. You're a neighbor.

Unfortunately, we have witnessed in our nation an alarming diminution of personal commitment to the wellbeing of others because we have rationalized that "letting government do it" is equal in moral weight to personally giving of our time, talent and treasure to our neighbors. In effect, we are becoming moral couch potatoes because we are no longer encouraged to exercise our values individually in daily actions of diligence in our work, commitment to our families, devotion in our houses of worship, and charity in our communities.

The impact of this shift in our thinking on charitable giving has practical as well as moral consequences. Arthur C. Brooks, author of *Who Really Cares: The Surprising Truth about Compassionate Conservatism*, found that people who believe that charity is an inherently governmental responsibility either restrict or curtail their charitable giving even if there is *only a promise* of government assistance.

In other words, those who believe in the forced redistribution of income through government are less likely to give to private charity even if the government isn't actually attempting to meet the need.

As private giving is withheld, charities find themselves dependent on government grants which bring with them the burden of various rules and regulations on how they distribute the funds, how they advise their beneficiaries and even who they must hire. Moreover, government disbursements to charity are insufficient to replace the loss of private funds. The net effect is that the people most in need of charitable assistance are getting less of it.

I've concluded from President Obama's own words that his Christian faith isn't the faith of our fathers, but rather a post-modern worldview rooted in relativism and secular humanism.

This false doctrine is designed for man's comfort rather than God's glory, because it allows its practitioners to follow the commands that appeal to them and ignore the ones that don't. President Obama's lead on discussing religion merely brought the same old religious socialists and their flawed theology out of the woodwork once again.

Should it matter to us that President Obama misrepresents his affinity with people of faith and distorts the teachings of the Bible, all to win our votes? Is there a Christian way to vote? Should we vote only for Christian candidates? Should we separate the practice of our faith from the exercising of our duties as citizens of a constitutional republic?

A lot of Christians think we should disengage from political activity because it corrupts our faith and reduces us to just another special interest group, rather than the transcendent presence God calls for us to be in the world. Political involvement, some say, makes us of the world rather than in the world. The former means we are taking on the character of the world. The latter says we are resident aliens on this planet, but it is not our home.

Secularists are doing everything in their power to eradicate every vestige of truth and faith from the public square, wielding as a sword the "separation of church and state," the false bromide of constricted hearts who seek to twist the Bill of Rights to suit aims other than maximizing the freedom of all Americans.

Aside from the fact this phrase appears nowhere in our Constitution or the Bill of Rights, these documents are, in all instances, intended not to place constraints on a free people, but on government itself. It is no accident that the freedom of assembly and petition stand alongside the free exercise of religion in the First Amendment.

The Establishment Clause prevents government from creating a state religion. It was never intended to restrict the rights of people of faith to express their beliefs, assemble in defense of their values or petition their government for consideration of their principles when crafting laws. It was meant to keep government from imposing on the people some dogma to which all would be beholden.

Thomas Jefferson's 1802 letter to the Danbury Baptists, which speaks of "a wall of separation between Church and State," was written to assuage their fears that the government might institute a state religion and restrict their religious liberties.

Enemies of faith, however, are doing just that with their insistence that the mere utterance of faith-based language or displays of religious symbols at public venues, constitutes the establishment of a state church. Such nonsense is propagated by the media, academia and the entertainment industry, and the end result is that liberty is constrained, not government as our founders intended.

Until government at any level makes it compulsory for me to attend a specific church, read a particular religious text, pray a certain prayer or practice specific religious rituals, then no church has been established and I'm as free as the next person to express my faith anywhere in the land. Get behind me, Satan!

The argument that "you can't legislate morality" is a canard as well. As St. Paul says: "All things are lawful, but not all things are profitable. All things are lawful, but not all things edify." [z]

Yet nearly every law takes a stand on a moral question. The law encourages or discourages specific behavior, thereby declaring that behavior "right" or "wrong." If the law couldn't "legislate morality," then we would have no laws against murder, stealing, lying or cheating. This point is so obvious it makes me wonder why it's even a matter of debate.

Those who object to people of faith petitioning their government for laws that reflect their natural moral beliefs are standing on shaky ground because there is a collective judgment of "right" or "wrong" behind every law.

As you might have surmised by now, tackling the thorny question of faith's role in a secular society has been a lifelong obsession for me, and that is because it's personal. I've been trying since the days of my youth to reconcile the competing passions of politics and Christ in my own life.

The times when I've been fully engaged in one passion, it's usually at the expense of the other. In the years when my faith was flagging, politics consumed me. When I was disillusioned with politics, I fully immersed myself in the church.

---

[z] 1 Corinthians 10:23.

Those times were fleeting, however. For the most part, politics and faith have exerted an equally compelling yet seemingly conflicting pull on my life.

Because of my personal struggle with this question, the movie *Amazing Grace*, chronicling the life of British Member of Parliament William Wilberforce, had great appeal to me. Wilberforce waged a lifelong battle to abolish the slave trade and, eventually, slavery itself in Great Britain.

Wilberforce was an up-and-coming young British politician, a stirring and accomplished orator with a bright future. Things changed, however, and in the movie, his butler finds him one day sitting in the middle of a meadow contemplating nature:

Richard the Butler: "You found God, sir?"

William Wilberforce: "I think He found me. You have any idea how inconvenient that is? How idiotic it will sound? I have a political career glittering ahead of me, and in my heart I want spider's webs."

Later, Wilberforce and his best friend, William Pitt, the youngest prime minister in British history, entertain several members of the abolitionist movement at Wilberforce's home. They are knowledgeable of his passion for their cause, his considerable political skills and his dilemma in reconciling his political career and his faith:

Thomas Clarkson: "We understand that you are having difficulty deciding whether to do the work of God or the work of a political activist."

Hannah More: "We humbly suggest you can do both."

I can't tell you how stirred I was by this brief scene in a movie. It summed up the challenge of my life and the response required of me. I've always thought back to it whenever I doubted myself or the course I'm taking.

Rick Boxx, the president of the Integrity Resource Center, a ministry dedicated to "restoring integrity and faith at work," is emphatic about the role of the Christian in the world. He said:

Many followers of Jesus Christ operate under the belief that value in God's eyes comes only from entering "full-time ministry." In essence, this means leaving their business or professional jobs to pursue careers directly affiliated with churches, mission agencies or "parachurch' ministries. In many cases, unfortunately, this is a tragedy that results in a terrible waste of gifts, expertise and experience.

God has made each of us with unique talents and has given us the opportunity to develop distinctive skills. When we mistakenly come to the conclusion that only missionaries or pastors have special, high callings from God, we miss His best for our lives. As a result, we may either leave work where God could have used us in extraordinarily fruitful ways for His purposes or, plagued by the feeling that our work is not important in God's grand scheme, we underutilize the gifts we have received.

In his first letter to the church in the ancient city of Corinth, the apostle Paul wrote, "Only let each person lead the life that the Lord has assigned to him, and to which God has called him. This is my rule in all the churches (1 Corinthians 7:17)."

Imagine a world in which everyone that claimed allegiance and devotion to Jesus Christ—called "Christians" in the Bible—served only as pastors and missionaries. Who would reach the people in the workplaces of the world? Who would provide the food, shelter, clothing, and other necessities that are essential for carrying out God's plan? Who would start businesses or lead our governments? To withdraw from being an integral, contributing part of the so-called "secular" work world (the Bible makes no such distinction) would be disastrous. Even worse, to do so is not God's plan.[23]

Therefore, the Christian citizen must be a Christian regardless of the endeavors in which he or she is engaged. As I'm fond of saying, "It's not just a Sunday thing—it's an everyday thing." Beware of those who say their faith teaches them one thing yet their actions support another. If their actions don't reflect their true beliefs, they are hypocrites.

For example, how many times have you witnessed politicians who claim the Catholic faith use the contrived logic of "separation of church and state" in attempts to justify abortion, embryonic stem cell research or same-sex 'marriage'? Maria Shriver Schwarzenegger, wife of California governor Arnold Schwarzenegger and member of the famed Kennedy clan, uses the term "cafeteria Catholic" to describe herself and other nominal Catholics who accept some teachings of their church but not all of them.

When running for vice president, Sen. Joe Biden tried to defend his pro-abortion record in Congress by stating that he believes the teachings of his Catholic faith that life begins at conception but thinks it "inappropriate" to "impose that judgment on others... in a pluralistic society." So the archbishop of Washington, DC, Donald W. Wuerl, weighed in.

"Defense of innocent human life is not an imposition of personal religious conviction but an act of justice," said Archbishop Wuerl.

I often wonder if such politicians ever pause to think about facing God on the day of judgment. Do they imagine that He will embrace them and say, "Well done, my good and faithful servant"[aa]?

To the contrary. After all, He gave them the power to protect little children and they not only failed to use it, but facilitated the killing of millions. I simply can't grasp their thinking.

Once I resolved that I could serve God in the political arena, I surrendered my worldview to His. The deepening of my Christian faith profoundly affected my politics, yet many people with whom I share Christian values and devotion hold completely different political positions than mine.

A black conservative friend of mine, Hassan Nurullah, had an experience similar to mine when he came to Christ. While I reverted to Christianity and dove deeper into it, Hassan came from a place farther away from it. He was raised a Muslim.

Nevertheless, once Hassan reached his adult years, he was compelled to seek truth. After much study, reflection and prayer, he believed that Christ was indeed "the way, the truth and the life." Consequently, as a Christian, Hassan reexamined everything and found his liberal political beliefs totally incompatible with his faith. As he explained:

The Bible says that when you accept Christ as your Lord and Savior, you take on the mind of Christ, that He performs a spiritual circumcision of the heart, that He replaces your heart of stone with one of flesh. This was certainly true in my case. I began to see the world in an entirely different light, it was as if scales literally fell from my eyes and I was seeing the world for the very first time.

[aa] Matthew 25:23 (New American Bible, 2003 © Libreria Editrice Vaticana).

*An unforeseen by-product of that new sight was a
fundamental change in my politics.*[24]

Consequently, Hassan said, "I haven't been able to
figure out how to be both a Christian and a supporter of
the Democratic Party."[25] Like me, Hassan is frustrated
by the people in the black community who nod their
heads vigorously in church as the pastor decries the
sin sweeping our nation. "Yet," Hassan wrote, "when
choosing political leaders, instead of applying the principles we say we believe in, time after time, we vote for
the exact opposite."[26]

In my opinion, far too many professed Christians
advocate a worldly agenda over the will of God. I'm often
reminded of Christ's rebuke, "Why do you call Me, 'Lord,
Lord,' and do not do what I say?"[ab]

Many Christians make the mistake of embracing
the merciful and loving Christ Who cares for the poor
and oppressed, ignoring the fact He is also the holy and
almighty One, Who commands us to be perfect as our
Father in heaven is perfect.

The same Jesus Who tells us to serve the poor also
commands us to refrain from sexual relations beyond a
loving marriage between a man and a woman—whether
it's adultery or premarital sex, including same-sex
unions.

Jesus commands us to defend the oppressed, yet
unborn children are the most oppressed among us. If
anything, children hold a special place in God's Kingdom
and so He says, "Let the little children come to Me, and
do not hinder them, for the kingdom of God belongs to
such as these."[ac]

And yes, unborn children are precious in the sight
of God. In the Bible, whose primary author is the Holy

[ab] Luke 6:46.

[ac] Matthew 19:14.

Spirit, God uses the same word to describe a baby before and after birth. In sacred scripture, the Lord speaks throughout the Bible of calling on His people and forming them and knowing them while they were in the womb.

From the beginning, God has been clear about the definition of marriage and the personhood of the unborn child. Combining the accounts of Apostles Matthew and Mark, note what Christ told the Pharisees when they tried to trick Him into justifying a liberal interpretation of divorce:

> *Some Pharisees approached him, and tested him, saying, "Is it lawful for a man to divorce his wife for any cause whatever?"*[ad]
>
> *He said to them in reply, "What did Moses command you?"*
>
> *They replied, "Moses permitted him to write a bill of divorce and dismiss her."*
>
> *But Jesus told them, "Because of the hardness of your hearts he wrote you this commandment. But from the beginning of creation, 'God made them male and female. For this reason a man shall leave his father and mother (and be joined to his wife), and the two shall become one flesh.' So they are no longer two but one flesh. Therefore what God has joined together, no human being must separate."*
>
> *In the house the disciples again questioned him about this. He said to them, "Whoever divorces his wife and marries another commits adultery*

[ad] Matthew 19:3 (Mark 10:2), NAB.

against her; and if she divorces her husband and marries another, she commits adultery."[ae]

Jesus seemed almost incredulous that these learned religious men didn't understand God's Word concerning marriage, even when stated so clearly.

God's Word is also crystal clear about the value He places on His most prized creatures. Jesus didn't have to mention abortion in the Bible because His Father already established that He is in communion with us before we are born:

Before I formed you in the womb I knew you, And before you were born I consecrated you...[af]

Similarly, the story of the meeting between Mary, who was pregnant with Jesus Christ, and her cousin Elizabeth, carrying the baby who would grow up to be St. John the Baptist, makes the personhood of the children they are carrying quite apparent:

Now at this time Mary arose and went in a hurry to the hill country, to a city of Judah, and entered the house of Zacharias and greeted Elizabeth. When Elizabeth heard Mary's greeting, the baby leaped in her womb; and Elizabeth was filled with the Holy Spirit. And she cried out with a loud voice and said, "Blessed are you among women, and blessed is the fruit of your womb! And how has it happened to me, that the mother of my Lord would come to me? For behold, when the sound of your greeting reached my ears, the baby leaped in my womb for joy. And blessed is she who believed

---

[ae] Mark 10:2-12 (Matthew 19:4-9), NAB.
[af] Jeremiah 1:5.

that there would be a fulfillment of what had been spoken to her by the Lord. "[ag]

I love the imagery of the unborn John the Baptist hearing the voice of the mother of Jesus and leaping with joy because he knew he was in the presence of the One to Whom his entire life would be dedicated. The Bible makes a firm statement about the consciousness and emotion in this unborn child, characteristics of a living human being.

Until our self-glorifying culture took hold, there was little to no dispute among Christians about the sanctity of the developing human inside the mother, and Christians understood that killing an unborn child was an assault on the very work of God, Who in the words of the Psalmist 'knit us together' in the womb.

I suppose if Mary lived in modern-day America, her contemporaries would be harassing her to have an abortion so she could get on with her life without being "punished with a baby," as then-Sen. Barack Obama put it in March 2008 campaign speech at Johnstown, Pennsylvania.

This same man thanked a Planned Parenthood audience in July of 2007 "for all the work that you are doing... for men who have enough sense to realize you are helping them all across the country."[ah, 27]

"Helping them" in what way? By killing the babies they helped to create, absolving them of the consequences of sexual intercourse, and essentially sanctioning the sexual exploitation of women?

God knew what He was doing when He gave the world His Son in first-century Bethlehem.

James Sherley, a prominent stem cell scientist and medical doctor, was deeply concerned about the

---

[ag] Luke 1:39-45.

[ah] Planned Parenthood also endorsed Obama for president.

prospect of Obama being elected president. Sherley, who also happens to be black, wrote, "The clarion credo of the Abolitionists who upended slavery in our great nation must be applied to the unborn: 'None of us are truly free, unless we are all free.' This transformative ideal of human beings must apply to us at all stages of our existence, including embryonic and prenatal, if we want to become the nation of truly free women and truly free men."[28]

It is a sin for us to be timid or muted when it comes to abortion and homosexuality, and we are really pressing our luck when we try to defend our positions by insisting the Bible doesn't really condemn homosexuality or even mention abortion, or dismissing the parts of the Bible with which we don't agree or understand. That's the theological equivalent of poking a sleeping bear with a stick—the outcome is probably not going to be pretty.

Standing firm for God on these issues doesn't absolve us from treating people who disagree with us "with gentleness and reverence," to use the words of the apostle Peter. Jesus had great compassion for sinners and forgave those who sought His grace, but He also warned them to "sin no more."

If, however, a sinner is unrepentant and incorrectly invokes God's love to shield himself or herself from criticism, if someone denies what God's Word teaches, then we must not yield. God is a loving parent but, like any parent, He holds us accountable for our statements and actions. His love does not excuse us from striving to be holy as He is holy.

This disconnect between faith and political action is most pronounced in the black community, where faith is still a powerful influence. To be fair, black people are not the only ones who proclaim Christ as Lord and Savior, yet don't reflect the influence of their faith in their politics. I can think of no other demographic group, however, where the consequences of that separation are so catastrophic.

Abortion is the single biggest killer of black Americans ever and there is no return on our community's grisly investment of billions of dollars in the abortion industry. In its scale and focus, it is nothing less than racial genocide, and we are willing participants in our own destruction.

As Dr. Sherley said, the parallels between slavery and abortion are stark. The business of slavery involves some human beings thinking they can own and violently abuse others. Worse yet, the abortion industry dehumanizes mothers and their babies in attempts to justify the most egregious of human actions. Therefore, I sincerely ask my black brothers and sisters: How is it that we can rationalize the ultimate violence of abortion in the name of the poor, the community or the national economy? Black people should be at the forefront of defending our children. Instead, the majority of us are sleeping with the enemy.

Government social programs, however well-intentioned, have diminished our self-sufficiency and devalued the black family, just as the late Daniel Patrick Moynihan predicted in 1965.

Moreover, the intrusive hand of government in our communities has not only not solved the crushing problems of poverty and crime in our inner cities, it has made them worse by crippling the institutions that sustained us in the past, not just the family but also the neighborhoods and the local church.

The cultural attacks on traditional marriage, beginning with the sexual revolution in the 1960s, have removed the stigma previously associated with single motherhood, making out-of-wedlock births in the black community the overwhelming norm rather than the exception. Statistics prove that children born into single-parent families are more likely to grow up poor, uneducated, homeless and engaged in crime, perpetuating the cycle of despair. The devastating impact on the black community of 72% of all black children being born without a father in the home is undeniable.

The crumbling of our culture, previously built around strong families and neighbors with Christ and His church in the center, has us directing our anger and frustration at one another. Is the 94% black-on-black murder rate not enough to shock us to our senses?

Our fight to be recognized as equal partners in the American Dream has taken a wrong turn somewhere. It seems perverse that, somehow, we had more two-parent families, less black-on-black crime and more neighbors helping neighbors during the worst days of Jim Crow than we do today. We have become more dependent than independent, placing our faith in faceless, soulless institutions rather than God, family and our own individuality.

The shackles of slavery and institutionalized discrimination weighed heavily on us, but the paternalism of modern liberalism, which places us in the role of helpless or incompetent victim and government as benevolent dictator, brings its own chains. In fact, the consequences of liberalism may be worse in the long run because it binds the mind and soul, restraining us from being the victors God says we are.

The Bible casts government not as our savior, but as a protector and enforcer—and nothing more. As St. Paul says:

> *For rulers are not a cause of fear for good behavior, but for evil. Do you want to have no fear of authority? Do what is good and you will have praise from the same; for it is a minister of God to you for good. But if you do what is evil, be afraid; for it does not bear the sword for nothing; for it is a minister of*

God, an avenger who brings wrath on the one who practices evil.[ai]

The role of government is to "bear the sword," to defend us against our enemies, ensure public safety, protect our unalienable rights and enforce justice for all its citizens. George Washington declared, "Government is not reason. It is not eloquence. It is force, like fire a dangerous servant and a fearful master." By asking government to be our provider as well as our protector, we are assigning to it a role for which it is not designed and for which it is ineffective.

Blacks who believe they owe their allegiance to the federal government because of its intervention on their behalf against slavery and discrimination are missing this point. Government's intervention when justice is denied is a constitutional duty, not a gift that was given to us.

My wife doesn't reward me for household chores—they are my obligation for living in a shared household. Neither do I reward government for doing its job, nor should you.

There is no room in our hearts for two masters and I choose the One that wants to set me free over the ones who want to keep me in the fold for no good purpose other than their own survival. Dr. Martin Luther King, Jr. once declared:

As Christians we must never surrender our supreme loyalty to any time-bound custom or earth bound idea, for at the heart of our universe is a higher reality—God and His kingdom of love—to which we must be conformed.

At the end of the day, this is the guidepost by which I determine my ultimate loyalty:

[ai] Romans 13:3-4.

If it is disagreeable in your sight to serve the LORD, choose for yourselves today whom you will serve: whether the gods which your fathers served which were beyond the River, or the gods of the Amorites in whose land you are living; but as for me and my house, we will serve the LORD.[aj]

[aj] Joshua 24:15.

-13-

This Is My Country

*"The government gives them the drugs, builds
bigger prisons, passes a three-strike law, and then
wants us to sing 'God Bless America.'No, no, no.
Not 'God Bless America'—'God Damn America!'
That's in the Bible, for killing innocent people. God
damn America for treating her citizens as less than
human. God damn America as long as she keeps
trying to act like she is God and she is supreme!"
~ Rev. Jeremiah Wright*

Black people aren't perceived as patriotic, at least
not in the commonly accepted sense of the term. I
suspect that most blacks will say they love their country,
but it's a qualified love, one that hasn't forgotten the
betrayals of the past and is reluctant to trust again for
fear of heartbreak.

It is in that context that the Rev. Jeremiah Wright
exploded onto the national consciousness in the midst of
the 2008 election. In addition to being Barack Obama's
pastor and mentor, Rev. Wright inspired the title of
Obama's book, *The Audacity of Hope.*

Wright didn't become a campaign issue until the
media began to report on excerpts from some of his sermons in which he railed against white people, berated
and cursed America for its sins, and implied that the
terrorist attacks of September 11, 2001, were justified,
declaring in the words of the late Malcolm X, "America's
chickens are coming home to roost."

Obama quickly distanced himself from Rev. Wright's comments and used them as the springboard for a major speech on race in America, "A More Perfect Union."

Some declared the speech brilliant and a major step forward in race relations. I simply thought he was trying to save his political bacon by rationalizing his attendance at Trinity United Church of Christ for 20 years, rather than walking out the minute Rev. Wright started spewing hate from the pulpit.

When Oprah Winfrey moved to Chicago, she was just another up-and-coming black professional and she began attending Trinity United. Eventually, when she rose to stardom, Winfrey reportedly left the church because of Jeremiah Wright. It seems she didn't want to risk offending her multi-racial audience.

Admittedly, my perspective on this topic is colored by my own experiences. Unlike Obama, I left the church altogether for over a decade because of a racist statement from the pulpit, and the words this pastor used were much more nuanced than Wright's diatribes. I believed then, and I believe now, that black liberation theology is a misrepresentation of the Gospel of Christ. Add to that the taking of the Lord's name in vain while cursing America and I wouldn't have spent a minute listening to such vitriol.

I remember Sen. Obama's speech more for how he threw his maternal grandmother under the bus, accusing her of latent racism characteristic of "a typical white person." Political analyst and journalist Taylor Marsh, among others, took offense at his inference that whites typically, albeit unconsciously, harbor racial fears. In the Huffington Post, she wrote:

It's becoming more apparent why Sen. Obama didn't leave Rev. Wright's church, as well as continued his relationship with him. The truth is that racism works both ways and some of us blue collar folks don't appreciate being called racist by someone who has his own problems with race he is obviously in denial about.[ak]

Over time, Rev. Wright continued to speak his mind, much to Sen. Obama's chagrin, and eventually the candidate had to sever his relationship with Wright and Trinity United Church of Christ. Obama had spent a lot of precious political capital to create an image of himself as a post-racial candidate and he couldn't have Rev. Wright's bigotry tarnishing that image.

I still go back to the fact he spent two decades in that church and I have a theory as to why he did, which I'll explain later.

Sen. Obama's speech on race revealed the historical and ongoing tension in the black community between America's ideals and her actions when it comes to racial equality. Even former Secretary of State Condoleezza Rice, then the highest-ranking black official in the federal government, thought Obama's statements brought out a necessary truth about the relationship between blacks and their country. She said:

> *There is a paradox for this country and a contradiction of this country and we still haven't resolved it... but what I would like understood as a black American is that black Americans loved and had faith in this country even when this country didn't love and have faith in them, and that's our legacy.*[29]

The conflict between the promise and the reality of America within the black community led to two group characteristics that may have aided in our survival during our darkest days as slaves and second-class citizens, but which I believe are now millstones around

---

[ak] March 20, 2008.

our necks that threaten to drag us to the depths of the sea—collectivism and victimization.

The history between black and white Americans is unlike that of any other demographic group. It dates all the way back to 1619 in Jamestown, Virginia, when the first Africans were brought to the English colony as indentured servants. Hundreds of years of slavery, institutionalized discrimination, and economic and social disparities between blacks and whites resulted in a collective worldview among American blacks.

This approach helped to shelter black families, churches and communities during the dark days of post-Reconstruction America leading up to the 1960s civil rights movement. Over time, group identity also became a source of political and economic power for the black community as we discovered our ability to effect policy and preferential treatment by presenting our grievances as a group.

Finally, and most critical to race relations today, groupthink became a way to keep blacks and whites in line. This is where it has become a burden to our progress.

Not only do the majority of blacks view themselves as a group that thinks and acts as one, they also judge whites in the same way.

In the black collectivist worldview, it doesn't matter that an individual white person has never discriminated against black people. Some whites persecuted and discriminated against blacks throughout history, therefore all whites must bear the burden of sins committed by their ancestors or predecessors.

Whites as a group must be kept in a constant state of culpability for racism, fostering an unending need for redemption, and resulting in material compensation to the black community. Since there is no statute of limitations on white guilt, especially since it's the black community that gets to decide when or whether the debt has been paid, this can go on until either a new generation of blacks comes along that lacks the latent resentment borne of America's racist legacy, or a new generation of whites decides it's had enough and pushes back.

Blacks are also held to account if they do not subscribe to the collectivist worldview. Blacks like me, who view themselves as unique individuals first, and treat others the same way, are denigrated and shamed to get back in line. The power of groupthink is so great that many blacks will even give unction to white liberals who use racial epithets against us. Black collectivists and their white enablers pummel black conservatives like Sambo and Quimbo pummeled Tom in *Uncle Tom's Cabin*. It's ugly.

Whites critical of the black collectivist worldview are labeled racists; blacks who question it are called traitors, sellouts and much worse. Collectivism in the black community exploits white guilt and stifles black individualism.

I believe, however, with the passage of time and the progress our society continues to make in race relations, something has to give, especially in the afterglow of electing the nation's first black president.

In my opinion, carrying this constant burden of bitterness over past and perceived present racial wrongs is harmful to the black community and to our nation as a whole. We need to find a resolution for our own well-being, and it's not "letting them off the hook" to follow the advice of Christ and forgive as our Father in Heaven forgave us.

Those few in the black community who would continue to employ collectivism as a form of extortion—I call them "race pushers"—will not be able to exploit the good intentions of most white people for much longer.

If collectivism is the effect, victimization is the cause, the emotion that gives our collectivist behavior its legitimacy. Victimization places blacks in the position of the aggrieved and whites as the aggressors, and once it becomes a part of our racial identity, we effectively absolve ourselves of any responsibility for our circumstances or our actions.

Social scientist and author Shelby Steele addressed the issue head on in an article, "The Loneliness of the Black Conservative":

> *And what is this explanation of black group authority? In a word it is victimization. Not only is victimization made to explain the hard fate of blacks in American history, but it is also asked to explain the current inequalities between blacks and whites and the difficulties blacks have in overcoming them. Certainly no explanation of black difficulties would be remotely accurate were it to ignore racial victimization. On the other hand, victimization does not in fact explain the entire fate of blacks in America, nor does it entirely explain their difficulties today.*

The positioning of victimization as the sole reason for black problems in America, past and present, makes a healthy, respectful relationship between blacks and whites virtually impossible. As Steele says, "Whites agree to stay on this hook for an illusion of redemption, and blacks agree to keep them there for an illusion of power." This is a dysfunctional family on a national scale.

Collectivism and victimization are the reasons our government has struggled for decades to issue a formal apology to the black community for slavery and its aftermath. The fear in white circles was that an apology would provide blacks with the legal grounds to demand reparations from the federal government.

In the summer of 2008, the U.S. House of Representatives formally apologized to the black community for the sins of slavery, including the domestic terrorism of lynching by the Ku Klux Klan, and Jim

Crow laws. I wrote about it in a column called, "Apology Accepted":

I guess it was inevitable that the House's formal apology for slavery and institutionalized segregation would bring out calls once again for reparations. It seems that many black leaders don't believe reconciliation is possible without some price being paid by the oppressors. To them, an apology is hollow—I guess it's gotta hurt for them to believe they really mean it.

My humble opinion is that reparations won't solve anything and will further exacerbate racial tensions. Consider all the tough questions reparations would raise:

How does one assign a monetary value to the impact of slavery and institutionalized discrimination on a people?

How long should reparations be paid?

Should people like Oprah and Tiger Woods receive a reparations check when they're wealthier than most white people?

What about the white people who reject racism and have never practiced it but still have to pay for it?

In order to help pay for reparations, should the U.S. bill those African nations whose tribes captured and sold their enemies to slave traders?

How would we use our reparations checks? Would we use them to invest in our own businesses, home owner- ship or acquisition of stock to create wealth for ourselves and our families, or would we just spend the money and be no better off than before except we have more "stuff"?

Would reparations bring reconciliation or resentment?

We need to take a global view and consider the con- sequences of what we're asking. I for one am not willing to burn down the house I live in just to demonstrate my moral superiority over another. Humans have wronged one another since the dawn of time and I've never seen money right ancient wrongs or heal the wounds people carry in their hearts.

As a committed Christian, the Bible is my source for the answer to this difficult question. Reconciliation can only be achieved by forgiveness. We are to forgive even if those who have wronged us do not consider themselves in need of forgiveness. If those who have wronged us come to us in humility and repent, we are to show them the same grace that Christ showed us by forgiving us even while we were sinners.

Practically speaking, forgiveness is the only path forward. Forgiveness wipes the slate clean and opens the door to dialogue and increased trust. Our common goal ought to be working as one to help America realize the ideals that make her a beacon to the rest of the world, not promoting retribution through reparations. I accept the House's apology and hope the Senate will follow suit and ask the President to sign it as a formal proclamation of our government's commitment to racial healing going forward. In God's economy, humility and repentance are priceless.

I mentioned previously that I had my own theory about Barack Obama's two decades at Trinity United Church of Christ, and why he stayed despite the deplorable anti-American and anti-white rhetoric spewed by Rev. Wright.

It is this: Obama's attitude toward America is in complete harmony with the typical left-wing narrative about this country, so nothing he heard from Rev. Wright was inconsistent with his worldview.

He considers himself a "citizen of the world" first, a point of view certainly reinforced by his upbringing in Hawaii and Indonesia. To this, I offer the words of President Theodore Roosevelt in his speech at the Sorbonne in France in 1902:

I believe that a man must be a good patriot before he can be, and as the only possible way of being, a good citizen of the world... Now, this does not mean in the least that a man should not wish to good outside of his native land. On the contrary, just as I think that the man who loves his family is more apt to be a good neighbor than the man who does not, so I think that the most useful member of the family of nations is normally a strongly patriotic nation. So far from patriotism being inconsistent with a proper regard for the rights of other nations, I hold that the true patriot, who is as jealous of the national honor as a gentleman of his own honor, will be careful to see that the nations neither inflicts nor suffers wrong, just as a gentleman scorns equally to wrong others or to suffer others to wrong him.

As an adult, Obama associated and collaborated with some of this nation's more radical dissidents, such as the domestic terrorist Bill Ayers.

President Obama leads the political party which preaches that the natural and fundamental principles of America are broken and need to be fixed. The Democrats are obsessed with class, race, gender and sexual orientation. In President Obama's own words, Democrats are on "the right side of history."

Some of the people he has appointed or nominated to positions of responsibility in government hold radical views well outside the mainstream of American thought. If most Americans simply read with their own eyes or heard with their own ears the opinions these individuals have publicly expressed, they would be outraged at their contempt for this nation, and the fact they were selected to positions of influence in its government.

In an article I wrote called "Two Americas" (not to be confused with the "two Americas" purported by former Sen. John Edwards(D-NC)), I offered my opinion of what Obama and his contemporaries think of our nation:

The other America is a place where our nation has committed many sins abroad for which it must atone. The world's ills are attributable primarily to our moral failures and our lack of humility. We are feared rather than respected, loathed rather than loved.

To the other America, the evil is believing in objective truth and a natural order of things. The highest virtue is self-fulfillment, and those who have not realized their dreams are the victims of a nation of privileged people, generally white, who seek to acquire and hoard their riches from others, usually by unethical or illegal means.

Since capitalism is inherently corrupt and people are greedy, only government has the means and the compassion to help the disenfranchised in society. Redistribution of wealth is a moral imperative because those who have much would otherwise shut out those who have little or nothing.

The Constitution is a flawed document written by hypocrites who extolled the virtues of freedom while owning slaves. Therefore, it is ignored as a relic of the past, even as our elected officials take an oath to uphold it.

Only elites, primarily the liberal ones, from the worlds of law, entertainment or academia have the right answers. The rest of us are, to use one liberal's description, "angry, uneducated hillbillies." We are useful only to subsidize their careers with our paychecks so they can continue to mock and insult us.

Recalling the archetype of the "authentic black," I suppose the expectation is that I'm supposed to temper my passion for America with my knowledge of her tainted history and keep her under constant scrutiny because she is still an inherently racist, xenophobic and sexist nation.

In this day and age, I'm certainly not supposed to be a political conservative or a devotee of the Founding Fathers, that group of privileged white men whose lofty principles weren't manifest in their daily lives. After all, they owned slaves, stole land belonging to Native Americans and treated women as second-class citizens. According to the collectivist agenda, the authentic American black man must never forgive and never forget. Instead, he must characterize America's moves toward righteousness as grudgingly done only under duress.

I take the path of forgiveness and grace, so I'm an unabashed patriot when it comes to America. For me only God and family take precedence over my home country. I am proud to be an American, I am not the least bit ashamed of her and I thank the Lord every day for putting me here over all the other nations on earth. In "Two Americas," I offered my vision of America:

One America sees our nation as a "shining city on a hill," a force for good in the world, and richly blessed by God because we have used our power to advance freedom rather than tyranny, seeking only enough territory to bury our dead from the wars fought in foreign lands to save millions of people from oppression.

We are a people of character, and we believe there is good and evil in the world and that anyone with common sense knows the difference.

We are a people that care for one another and we are generous to the world, giving more private charity to other countries than any nation past or present. We are compassionate toward those who cannot help themselves and will help those who can to become productive and self-sufficient citizens. We believe that the true power of our nation is in its people and not in its government, and it is our emphasis on individual liberty and initiative that has made us strong.

Our systems of government and economics are the envy of the world, and our freedoms are a beacon to millions who came here, and continue to come, to realize their dreams of creating wealth for themselves and their families, or to worship in peace, or simply to breathe the rarified air of liberty. More people seek to come to America than to leave.

While we know we are not perfect, we have unceasingly strained toward the goal of living up to our Declaration of Independence, Constitution and Bill of Rights, three of the most transformative secular documents in world history.

With our combination of military might, the largest economy in world history, and a higher number of immigrants than any other nation that has ever existed, we believe that we are exceptional, and we are a stabilizing and comforting presence in the world. In short, we are proud of America and to be called Americans.

I gave years of my life in her defense as a member of the armed forces, as did my father before me, so I've always been immersed in the symbols and ceremony of my country—the uniform bedecked with American emblemology, the Stars and Stripes, the National Anthem, the marches, the patriotic speeches on Memorial Day, Veterans' Day, the Fourth of July, and so on.

When I lived overseas, either as a military dependent or an intelligence officer, I was always mindful of the fact that my words and actions reflected not only on me but also the United States of America and I tried to conduct myself accordingly.

For all the folks who think this country is irredeemably flawed, precious few of them ever actually go away to some other more enlightened land, wherever that may be. In fact, more people have emigrated from foreign lands to America than any other nation in history, and over a million people a year legally come to our country from distant shores. Over a million immigrants became American citizens in 2008.

Entertainers who use the bully pulpit with which they've been blessed to bash America are particularly loathsome to me. They went from waiting tables, playing in neighborhood bands or doing local dinner theater to the starry heights of fame and fortune because millions of ordinary Americans bought tickets to their movies, watched their TV shows, attended their concerts, bought their CDs or downloaded their MP3s. Yet they don't hesitate to mock and denigrate those same Americans for their heartland values, their faith or their love of country. They've forgotten the phrase "Only in America" and never stop for one minute to think of how blessed they are to live in a nation where they can find such success.

Why do I love America? Simply put, it was the first nation founded on the principle that each individual human being is precious in the sight of God. Everything good that has happened in America since its founding has been predicated on our constant striving toward that goal.

I don't see the abolition of slavery, women's suffrage, the end of Jim Crow laws and the ascension of a black man to the White House as steps taken reluctantly, but rather the inevitable consequence of a nation whose constitutional law is ordered to the dignity and worth of the individual human person.

Our Founding Fathers were troubled by slavery even as they drafted the U.S. Constitution, and although they made concessions in the interest of preserving the Union, they knew it was a moral evil that could not long survive in a nation founded in liberty. America's history tells me that its good-willed citizens are always straining, stretching and clawing toward the ideal under which our nation was founded, and we will not cease until that ideal has been reached.

Hence, all major religions of the world thrive here. Even our poor have a higher standard of living than billions of people worldwide. That is why immigrants, with their work ethic and entrepreneurial spirit, are more successful in America than in the great nations of Europe.

That is why my ascension as a black man in America isn't based on being in the right tribe, having the right bloodline or being in the majority or the faction with the most guns. I succeed in America because I matter as an individual and I am empowered to chart my own direction. As long as I play by the rules, there are thousands of fellow Americans, some I've not even met yet, who stand ready to help me and cheer me on.

It was America, not the supposedly more enlightened European or Asian nations, which elected a person of color to lead the most powerful, most prosperous, most influential nation that has ever existed on the planet. Am I better off in America than in any other country in the world, even as a black man? To quote a certain former governor of Alaska, "You betcha!"

Even as President Obama travels around the world apologizing for America's sins, a dubious exercise from my perspective as a veteran assigned to help defend freedom in foreign lands we liberated from tyranny, I have two observations of note. America, unlike empires past, never stays where it is not wanted and almost always leaves a nation better than it was when we first arrived.

From the shores of Normandy to the beaches of the south Pacific, most of the world owes its prosperity and freedom to the United States of America. Whatever the circumstances that led us to be where we are, certainly the people of our armed forces, if not the government, have always tried to do the right thing by our fellow human beings. We have generously given more in charity and shed more blood for the betterment of our world than any other nation and for that I make no apologies.

Former British Prime Minister Tony Blair said in a speech to British ambassadors in London:

I am not surprised by anti-Americanism; but it is a foolish indulgence. For all their faults and all nations have them, the U.S. are a force for good; they have liberal and democratic traditions of which any nation can be proud. I sometimes think it is a good rule of thumb to ask of a country: are people trying to get into it or out of it? It's not a bad guide to what sort of country it is.

It is a sobering sign when the chief executive of the nation from which America declared its independence 234 years ago understands the exceptional nature of America more than many of its own citizens. For me, America is John Winthrop's "shining city on a hill" and she stands as a beacon to human beings everywhere.

-14-

Not Their Cup of Tea

*"Let's be very honest about what this is about.
This is not about bashing Democrats. It's not about
taxes. They have no idea what the Boston Tea Party
was about. They don't know their history at all.
It's about hating a black man in the White House.
That is racism straight up. This is nothing but
a bunch of teabagging rednecks."*
~ Janeane Garofalo

It was a sun-splashed, unseasonably mild Sunday afternoon on March 22, 2009. Those of us who were gathered at the Solomons Pavilion in Maryland had no idea whatsoever of the controversy that awaited us in the months ahead.

Less than a month prior, a local attorney and some friends of his, together representing Republicans, Democrats and independents, had approached the chairman of the Calvert County Republican Central Committee about hosting a rally to protest the $787 billion economic stimulus package and the $3.5 trillion budget submitted by President Obama. In an email message, the attorney wrote, "I have been watching on the news the growing taxpayer revolt expressed in the form of 'tea party' protests" and he wondered if we could do something similar.

Taxpayer frustration had been growing since October 2008, when President Bush signed the Emergency Economic Stabilization Act of 2008 into law. Despite predictions from elected officials and Wall Street of a financial collapse with global consequences if the federal government didn't act, the American people were opposed to what appeared to be a bailout of the U.S. financial system to shield these companies from the consequences of their own mismanagement.

Protests against the bailout occurred in over 100 cities across the country on September 25, 2009 and constituent phone calls and email messages to members of Congress were overwhelmingly in opposition to the bailout. A *USA Today*/Gallup poll showed that 56% of Americans wanted another solution, and 11% wanted them to take no action at all. Ironically, these early protests brought free-market conservatives and anti-corporate liberals together, all united in their opposition to the mantra that these financial firms were "too big to fail."

Sen. John McCain, locked in a tight battle for the presidency with then-Sen. Barack Obama, suspended his campaign and rushed back to Washington to engage in the legislative debate over the bailout. The fact he ended up voting in favor of it was, in my opinion, the final nail in the coffin for an estimated 7 million conservative voters who had voted for Bush in 2004, but stayed home on Election Day 2008 rather than vote for either candidate.

The negative response to the proposal was so great that it initially failed to pass in Congress. It was revised, passed and quickly signed into law, thus planting the seed for an unprecedented grassroots uprising unlike any seen in living American history.

As he was leaving office, President Bush declared in an interview, "I've abandoned free-market principles to save the free market system." To most conservatives, this was the final betrayal by a man who had declared himself a "compassionate conservative," but who, after eight years of record spending increases and expanded government, had left the conservative brand in shambles.

If anyone thought President Obama would take a slow and prudent approach to spending after the budget-busting deficits of his predecessor, they were soon disabused of that notion. Talk of economic stimulus packages, mortgage bailouts and auto industry bailouts ran rampant in the nation's capital, and one observer had seen and heard enough.

On February 19, 2009, Rick Santelli, an on-air editor for television business channel CNBC, began ranting from the floor of the Chicago Board of Trade about the government bailing out irresponsible homeowners who bought more house than they could afford.

To the applause of the listening traders, he accused the government of "promoting bad behavior" and declared, "We're thinking of having a Chicago Tea Party in July. All you capitalists that want to show up to Lake Michigan, I'm gonna start organizing." A movement that had passion but no form had found its rallying cry.

I cite this history for the simple reason that opponents of the burgeoning Tea Party movement often ask, "Where were you when Bush was running up record deficits?"

The answer is that we were indeed frustrated with President Bush's $700 billion bailout, and we made our displeasure known through protests, phone calls and emails to our legislators, tactics not dissimilar to those we use today.

We also delivered a message when 7 million conservatives didn't vote for John McCain in November. Had he shown some fiscal responsibility and voted against the bailout, he might have persuaded enough of us that his conservative credentials were bona fide, and that could have changed the outcome of the election.

The reaction of Tea Party protesters to President Obama's agenda is proportionate to the unprecedented levels of spending by his administration. The budget deficit in President Obama's first year in office was $1.4 trillion, the largest on record, and he is expected to break that record in fiscal year 2010. Based on the budget he submitted to Congress, trillion-dollar deficits will be the norm for the remainder of his current term. The humorist Will Rogers once said, "If you find yourself in a hole, stop digging." Not only is President Obama continuing to dig, but he's using a bigger shovel. It's his policies and his introduction of the phrase "trillion-dollar deficit" into the ongoing budget debate, with all the consequences such astronomical spending entails, that turned a smoldering dissatisfaction into a raging inferno of action.

We managed to pull the first Tea Party protest in Maryland together on pretty short notice, but we had no idea who would turn up on a Sunday afternoon to wave signs and dump fake boxes of tea into the Patuxent River (with fishing wire attached, of course, so they could be retrieved and the environment preserved). Prior to the event, the local GOP chairman fretted in an email message to the attorney and other prominent county Republicans:

> *As you know, like most citizens, Republicans generally focus on their families, work, hobbies, etc. and tend not to be active 'protestors' beyond sending an e-mail, writing a letter, complaining to fellow Republicans, etc.*

Much to our surprise, however, when things kicked off, we had an enthusiastic and energized crowd that the local sheriff estimated at about 540 people. They came from the District of Columbia, northern Virginia and all over Maryland. I was the master of ceremonies, orchestrating the music, guest speakers and the symbolic dumping of tea into the water at the end. We invited selected local Democratic Party officials to join our protest, but they either declined or never responded.

One of our speakers was Charles Lollar, a friend and the chairman of the Charles County Republican Central Committee. His stirring speech electrified the crowd. This charismatic and engaging businessman, former Marine, and husband and father to four girls would go on to become a popular presence at several subsequent Tea Party rallies, including the largest one to date, held in Washington, DC on September 12, 2009.

Charles and I stood out from the crowd at Solomons that day because we were the only black people present. It didn't concern us one bit at the time, because we were all united in our opposition to runaway spending, higher taxes and encroaching government at the federal and state level.

Annapolis, the capital of Maryland, is a microcosm of the mess in Washington, DC. Its $2 billion annual budget deficits threaten our economy and our quality of life. The governor and the Democratic super-majority in the General Assembly keep spending indiscriminately and raised our taxes to where we have the fourth highest combined state and local tax burden in the nation. So Maryland citizens have ample reason to take to the streets.

The handmade signs were creative and many were funny. We awarded a cash prize to the boy whose sign declared he was already over $30,000 in debt despite being only 12 years old. As I went through the crowd afterwards to thank them for coming, I met an elderly lady seated in a chair, and I knelt down to say hello and thank her for being there. She whispered into my ear, "I've never done anything like this my entire life, but I'm angry and I have to do something."

This is a theme that personifies the Tea Party movement—everyday Americans too busy with life to protest, but who have suddenly been awakened by the magnitude of current political events and spurred into doing something they've never done before.

We weren't as skilled or experienced in the art of protest as our liberal counterparts. It was only the second protest rally I'd attended in my life, and this one and the other I attended previously had all the edginess of a high school pep rally. We certainly weren't violent or destructive to private property as those we typically witnessed at protests over world monetary policy, immigration, "gay rights" and other liberal causes. Nonetheless, we came out and made our voices heard.

Not everyone was pleased. A couple of local talk radio hosts came and were dismayed by the prevalence of the Republican Party at the event. I called into their show to explain that we were asked by a tri-partisan group of ordinary citizens to host the event and that we opened it to everyone, but many conservative Democrats were fearful of showing up. We noted their complaints and, in subsequent rallies at Solomons, non-partisan free-market and individual liberty advocates such as Americans for Prosperity hosted the events.

Because of our Tea Party success, Charles Lollar and I were invited to speak at a Tea Party rally at the City Dock in Annapolis on April 15th, 2009—Tax Day. Similar rallies were to take place all around the country.

The rally in Annapolis was organized by Aaron Jones, a young man and small business owner from Salisbury, Maryland, who, with his ponytail and goatee, was a somewhat unconventional looking organizer for an anti-spending, anti-tax, pro-free market rally. He was just another reminder to me of the true grassroots, mainstream nature of this movement, and what it lacks in formal organization or leadership, it more than makes up for it in commitment and passion.

Unlike the mild, sunny weekend day that greeted our first Tea Party, it was cold and the wind was driving the rain into us like bullets. The water whipping off the

Chesapeake Bay only made matters worse. I was not dressed appropriately for the weather, so I was wet and shivering by the time I left two hours later.

The weather didn't discourage people from showing up. Over 2,000 stood there as the wind and rain pounded us and more were coming from the Navy-Marine Corps Memorial Stadium where they parked and were to be delivered to the City Dock by bus. The mayor of Annapolis, apparently not amused by our rally, had only two buses running to deliver people to the rally site. Undaunted, many of them walked from the stadium to the City Dock.

Families with children, students, housewives, businessmen—we were as mainstream a crowd as you could imagine. They came carrying homemade signs, American flags or the emerging banner of the Tea Party movement, the Gadsden "Don't Tread on Me" flag. All of us were energized by our newfound voice in the political arena despite the nasty weather.

I remember wondering at the first Tea Party if the people were truly committed to the Tea Party movement's goals of individual liberty, federalism, a smaller, less intrusive federal government, lower taxes, reduced spending, and fiscal responsibility and accountability. That afternoon in Annapolis left no doubt in my mind.

As I drove home afterwards, I got my first indication of how the rest of the nation reacted to the Tea Party protests.

A reporter called me and asked if I'd heard that the Maryland National Guard was on alert because of the Tea Party rallies that day. He referenced the Department of Homeland Security's (DHS) memo, branding anti-government protesters as "right-wing extremists" capable of violent attempts to overthrow the government, as the basis for the alert.

I laughed. In my remarks at the Tea Party rally, I mentioned how, as a member of the transition team that helped to establish DHS, I was disappointed they were taking their focus off of the radical Islamic terrorist threat and meddling with harmless domestic political demonstrators. That wouldn't be the last time this peaceful, mainstream movement would be accused of inciting violence.

As I followed the mainstream media reports on the Tea Party rallies across the country, I noted they fell into one of three categories:

Pretend it didn't happen – Most of the major national news outlets didn't even report on the Tea Party rallies. Instead, the typical last-minute rush to submit tax returns received more coverage. What is newsworthy about that?

Make fun of them – When the rallies were reported, it was usually to mock the protesters and their colonial theme or underreport the numbers of people participating to make the movement seem insignificant.

Demonize them – Some news outlets challenged the intent and purpose of the Tea Party rallies, declaring they were orchestrated by the Republican Party or the Fox News Channel to embarrass the new president.
A CNN reporter placed herself in the story by confronting Tea Party protesters in Chicago, her commentary dripping with barely disguised contempt for her interview subjects.

Another CNN personality used the word "teabagger," a vulgar sexual term, on the air to describe the Tea Party participants. This vulgarity became the preferred descriptor used by opponents of the movement, an obscene expression by the strident left to express their scorn for the common Americans in the Tea Party movement.

Regrettably, even the president of the United States called us "teabaggers" several times. And when he did, even naïve individuals like me, who had to have the connotation explained to us, understood what it meant.

The most shameful reaction, however, came from MSNBC, a news channel so deep in the tank for Obama during the 2008 presidential campaign that other journalists nicknamed it "The Obama News Network."

During an interview with MSNBC on-air personality Keith Olbermann, comedienne and actress Janeane Garofalo opened a Pandora's Box when she declared the motivation of the Tea Party protesters to be "racism straight up." Olbermann nodded in agreement with her accusation and, thanks to their scurrilous charge, the so-called post-racial era many proclaimed after Barack Obama's election was over mere months after it had begun.

As the months wore on and the Tea Party protests grew, frustrated Democrats spent their arsenal of insults in a futile attempt to discredit the movement. The protesters were, by turns, Astro-Turf (faux grass roots), Nazis, fascists, brownshirts, an angry mob and, in a *USA Today* editorial co-authored by Speaker of the House Nancy Pelosi (D-CA) and House Majority Leader Steny Hoyer (D-MD), "un-American."

The accusation of racism persisted, however, kept alive by the mainstream media's distorted focus on the outliers and fringe elements common to every mass movement and who, in this case, exploited the Tea Party rallies to express vile, racially-motivated criticisms of the president.

These few people are agitators, not representatives of the Tea Party movement. But they make great copy for the evening news and they feed the prejudice of everyone who wants to characterize the Tea Party movement as a potential lynch mob.

Frankly, while I'd like to see more black people at the Tea Party rallies, I think it's foolish for me or anyone else to expect that or to use the relative absence of black people to justify claims of racism.

If the president were a liberal white male attempting to enact the same game-changing agenda, the same people would be protesting against him. Under those conditions, would they still be considered racist?

Let's review the math. No Republican candidate for president has received more than 15% of the black vote since 1964. Blacks overwhelmingly identify with the Democratic Party and, in 2008, Barack Obama received a whopping 95% of the black vote. Given these statistics, why would anyone even expect to see a lot of black faces at a Tea Party rally?

MSNBC, the network that continues to keep the Tea Party racism charge alive, has no black news anchors or commentators. CNN is also very white. So does that make them racist? Of course not.

The reasons blacks aren't represented in large numbers at the Tea Party rallies are many and varied, but racism isn't one of them. I don't expect to see a lot of whites at NAACP conventions, but that doesn't mean I automatically make the leap to declaring it a racist organization (although I'm sure I could start an interesting discussion on that topic!).

Washington Post reporter Dana Milbank conceded that the movement wasn't inherently racist despite the narrative being pushed by the left and their friends in the media:

I bet 90% of the people there were normal and decent folks whose message had nothing to do with racism, anti-Semitism and genocide. This is probably the same proportion as at any political event, left or right.

Shannon Travis, a black CNN producer who traveled with the Tea Party Express, one of the many independent groups that comprise the Tea Party movement, made a similar observation:

There were a few signs that could be seen as offensive to African-Americans. But by and large, no one I spoke with or I heard from on stage said anything that was approaching racist. Almost everyone I met was welcoming to this African-American television news producer.

In his report, Travis "profiled African-Americans who are proud to be in the Tea Party's minority" and I'm sure he discovered, as Charles Lollar and I have from personal experience, that they were warmly received by their white fellow Tea Partiers.

Shannon Travis' declaration that "the stereotypes don't tell the whole story" was met with anger by opponents of the movement, including many media outlets. This is a strange reaction from supposedly objective media. CNN was accused of pandering for ratings, a charge it vehemently denied.

One of the reasons for the backlash might have been that the report followed an episode that was probably the zenith of the Tea Party racism narrative.

The weekend of March 20-21, 2010 marked the climactic debate in the U.S. House of Representatives on President Obama's signature program, the controversial overhaul of the nation's healthcare system.

Several Tea Party protests held during the week culminated in a large rally on Capitol Hill that began on Friday night and extended through the weekend. Passions were high and Republican legislators encouraged the Tea Party protesters to keep up the pressure, because the vote would decide the eventual fate of the bill that many had dubbed "Obamacare."

Several black members of Congress, who were either entering or leaving the Capitol at various times, walked a gauntlet of angry protesters and, by their account, all hell broke loose.

They said the word "nigger" was shouted at them multiple times by some in the crowd, and another said he was spat upon by one of the demonstrators. House Majority Whip James Clyburn (D-SC), a veteran of the civil rights movement, said, "I have heard things today that I have not heard since March 15, 1960, when I was marching to get off the back of the bus."

The mainstream press ran with this narrative like a dog snatching a steak off the grill, and the leftist blogosphere wasn't far behind.

What they didn't expect was to be challenged on their assertions. Multiple conservative outlets, reviewing numerous videos of the supposed shouting and spitting episodes, neither saw nor heard anything of the kind.

People in attendance refuted the allegations as well. Subsequent reports suggested the "spitting" was probably saliva inadvertently hitting the face of a member of Congress who came in close proximity to a shouting protester.

Andrew Breitbart, a conservative blogger and watchdog of the entertainment and news industries, offered a $100,000 donation to the United Negro College Fund if anyone could produce video evidence these events occurred. As of this writing, three months after the weekend in question, there are no takers.

Is it possible people in the crowd of thousands were shouting racial slurs? Given the fact even centrally organized and orchestrated large-scale protests have extremists in their midst, it's possible.

Where there orchestrated chants or outbursts by a large number of participants that could clearly be heard? I don't think so. Had that happened, I'm confident the vast majority of protesters would have shouted them down and put them in their place. When a protester inside one of the legislative office buildings shouted an anti-gay slur at Rep. Barney Frank (D-MA), he was immediately repudiated by the other protesters, with one shouting, "We don't need that!"

Even the *Washington Post* ombudsman, Andrew Alexander, said the allegations merited more reporting given the lack of video evidence and the insistence within the conservative blogosphere that the events were exaggerated or made up. Specifically addressing the spitting allegation, Alexander said:

> *With videos of the incident so prevalent on liberal and conservative Web sites, and with the question being so widely raised in the blogosphere and on cable channels, The Post was remiss in not providing clarity by quickly dissecting what happened.*

Were Rep. Clyburn, Rep. John Lewis (D-GA), a civil rights icon, and the other black legislators lying?

Here's what I think. Some of these men have stared down more mobs of angry white people than I ever have or will, and I have no doubt what they witnessed that sunny, unseasonably mild weekend in March brought back horrible memories from their pasts. To them, I imagine thousands of angry, mostly white protesters today don't look or sound a whole lot different than the crowds they encountered in the 1960s.

That said, their anger wasn't motivated by race. When you're being ignored or dismissed by the elected officials you empowered to act on your behalf, anger is the predictable outcome.

Our lawmakers were on the verge of enacting a controversial program that promised to place government firmly and permanently in the midst of the private, personal relationship between doctor and patient. This program promises to add trillions more to the already out-of-control budget deficit, which is already destined to burden our children and grandchildren for generations to come. Worst of all, individuals will be forced to buy health insurance or be punished by the government—which is a clear violation of our constitutional rights.

The people clearly expressed their opposition to Obamacare in the opinion polls and at the ballot box, with Scott Brown's stunning upset in Massachusetts putting a Republican in the seat the late Sen. Ted Kennedy had occupied since 1962. Sen. Brown had campaigned and won on the promise to be the 41st vote against government health care.

Despite all of this, not only were the Democrats charging ahead with their plans, they circumvented the normal legislative process for making a bill into law, bypassing the safeguards built into the system to prevent the federal government from enacting large-scale, potentially damaging legislation. In my opinion, the anger of the people is justified.

But it's not motivated by racism.

And what of the man who is the subject of these allegations, President Barack Obama? Does he believe that criticism of his policies is racially motivated?

On September 15, 2009, former President Jimmy Carter appeared on *NBC Nightly News* claiming that "an overwhelming portion" of the criticism directed at the president is because he's black. The very next day, White House Press Secretary Robert Gibbs said, "The president does not believe that that criticism comes based on the color of his skin."

Former President Bill Clinton, a Southerner like Carter, also took issue with the allegations. On CNN's *Larry King Live*,[al] he said:

[al] September 22, 2009.

I believe that some of the right-wing extremists which oppose President Obama are also racially prejudiced and would prefer not to have an African-American president.

But I don't believe that all the people who oppose him on health care—and all the conservatives—are racists. And I believe if he were white, every single person who opposes him now would be opposing him then.

Days before Clinton weighed in, President Obama did five TV interviews saying that he doubted the charges of racism. In two, he said the protestors were "anti-government."[30]

To CNN, he offered a more accurate assessment: "Are there people out there who don't like me because of race? I'm sure there are. That's not the overriding issue here."[31]

To NBC, he attributed the passion of his opponents to the ongoing debate on the proper role of government:

It's an argument that's gone on for the history of this republic, and that is, "What's the right role of government? How do we balance freedom with our need to look out for one another?"... This is not a new argument, and it always evokes passions.[32]

And to ABC News, the president admitted, "Are there some people who voted for me only because of my race? There are probably some of those too."[33]

My observation is that President Obama is a reluctant warrior and a bit of an opportunist when it comes to the topic of race. He is clearly uncomfortable casting issues in racial terms and there are only three conditions under which I've seen him invoke race.

He uses the issue of race when he needs to generate a large minority voter turnout. Witness his 2010 midterm elections video appeal to "young people, African-Americans, Latinos, and women who powered our victory in 2008 [to] stand together once again."[34]

The other time he discusses race is when he's backed into a corner, as he was during the 2008 campaign when the continuing controversy over the Rev. Jeremiah Wright's incendiary comments from the pulpit forced his hand.

In response, Obama delivered his famous campaign speech in Philadelphia on race in America. Although not explicitly stated, he and his campaign staff clearly hoped all the race talk would die down after he'd addressed it.

Finally, race becomes a hands-on topic for him when a friend is involved, as with his condemnation of the Cambridge, Massachusetts police department for their arrest of Harvard professor Henry Louis Gates at his own home.

Even in that incident, he quickly backed off his comment that the police acted "stupidly." He hastily arranged a beer summit at the White House between himself, Vice President Biden, Professor Gates and James Crowley, the Cambridge police officer who had arrested Gates for disorderly conduct.

President Obama self-identifies as "African-American" on his census form, but in background, temperament, tone and action, he demonstrates much more comfort and commonality with conventional left-wing causes than issues concerning most urban blacks.

He has come under criticism from black interest groups for not focusing on the disproportionate impact the current recession is having on the black community, and for the dearth of black appointees at the top of his administration.

A good example of his relative ambivalence on race is his recent nomination of Solicitor General Elena Kagan for the United States Supreme Court. She was selected over several more qualified candidates, including former

Georgia Supreme Court Chief Justice Leah Ward Sears, the first black woman to ascend to that position.

This may be a circumstance of ideological concerns outweighing racial solidarity. Although Justice Sears is a liberal jurist, she is also good friends with black conservative Supreme Court Justice Clarence Thomas, a pariah in the eyes of the black orthodoxy. The opportunity to have two black people, and the first black female justice ever, on the Supreme Court, apparently wasn't enough to sway him.

Political scientist and black political strategist Ron Walters said of Obama's Supreme Court appointment, "It is another one of those pin pricks where African-Americans are not happy with the president's decision. These things were inevitable, but they continue to happen. And this was just another one."[35]

Walters went on to say Obama's decision came from the "elite crowd of Harvard law school that's the other world that he's been traveling in since he was a very young person."[36] And he stressed:

Don't underestimate the strength of that culture because it is certainly there. And he is a part of that culture. As a matter of fact, I would dare say that he is more a part of that culture than he is of the civil rights culture.[37]

It's probably safe to conclude that President Obama doesn't share his supporters' conviction of the Tea Party movement's racist impulses. I would also suggest that he knows if he used the race narrative as a shield to avoid reproach, he would lose the respect of the people in the process. His post-racial credentials mean a lot to him.

As for me, I've spent more time "embedded" in the Tea Party movement than have the critics. I've spoken at four Tea Party rallies and attended many more, including the massive September 12, 2009 gathering in Washington which featured about half a dozen black speakers.

I know its leaders and I know the hearts and souls of the majority of the participants with whom I've had contact.

If I had encountered racism on a pervasive scale, I would have nothing to do with the movement. I know the leaders are attempting as best they can, within this decentralized grassroots movement minus hierarchical structure, to self-police. They've issued a number of public statements repudiating racist actions.

I have one more recollection of that first Tea Party in Maryland that stays with me. I was given a ride to the rally by a longtime friend, Theresa Mullen. Her husband, Gary, had been suffering from kidney disease for many years and it had reached the point where he could no longer do all the things he loved to do.

One of his favorite activities was creating handmade political signs to post in his yard or to use while sign waving. While he couldn't physically be there, he created a sign for Theresa to bring with her to the Solomons rally. Theresa thoroughly enjoyed the rally and was highly motivated to stay engaged in the Tea Party movement.

She and Gary had been active in more conventional ways in the past, serving as precinct chairpersons in the voting district where they lived, and participating in local Republican Party activities. That's not how I got to know them, however.

We met them through Chesapeake Church. Gary was actively involved with the church's drama ministry, The Edge, and performed for the children in Rainbowland Park, the children's ministry. He led the pre-teens and teens in the Parable Players drama ministry, and my daughters credit his attention and encouragement with leading them into the performing arts.

It was the Mullens' great American story of triumph over tragedy that most endeared me to them.

Theresa endured terrible abuse at the hands of her first husband. When she finally escaped from him, she found herself hungry, homeless and with two small children to care for.

Gary was a rebellious teenager with a drinking problem and a temper. He once told us about the time he awoke in a jail cell and had no idea how he ended up there.

Somehow, God brought these two broken souls together. Gary was totally devoted to Theresa's children even though they weren't his own, and this so endeared Gary to her that she knew she wanted to marry him.

He cleaned up his act and never drank again. Both of them dedicated their lives to Christ. They had two more children and raised a loving family with God at the center of their lives.

Gary eventually became an elder at our church, but he continued to serve in the various drama ministries and to serve the children of the church. He drove a trash truck for a living, and became famous at the local Christian radio station because he was always calling in for their various contests and giveaways while on the road.

When Gary and Theresa started a church home group for couples, we eagerly joined and began a journey with them and other couples that created a bond tighter than family. We share our lives together to this day.

When we were going through rough times, our home group was always there for us, and Gary and Theresa rescued us financially on more than one occasion when I was out of work.

Gary developed kidney disease a few years ago and it was debilitating enough to where he couldn't work for some time. He miraculously recovered, however, and was able to support his family again.

After a long stretch of relatively good health, the disease returned and Gary eventually learned he would need a kidney transplant to survive. He began a difficult and constricting regimen of home dialysis and he had to go on a restricted diet to manage his condition until a kidney donor could be found.

Through it all, he never stopped serving others, whether in our church, our community or our home group.

Because it would have been too difficult for him to endure the large crowds at the Tea Party rallies, he relied on Theresa and me to keep him up to speed on what happened—who spoke, how many people there were, that sort of thing. It was as if he lived through our experiences.

Gary was a good driver, so he often volunteered to drive the church's children to and from their field trips, whether it was to a ski resort in Pennsylvania or to downtown Washington, DC to feed the homeless.

It was on one such trip that he returned feeling seriously ill. He drove himself to the emergency room and was immediately placed in intensive care. All of us in his home group were concerned, but we thought it was just another indication of how important it was for him to get a kidney transplant as soon as possible.

He never got that chance. His body was ravaged by disease and he lapsed into a coma from which he never awoke. He was 47 years old and left behind Theresa, his wife of nearly 18 years, and their four children. Before Gary died, he saw his oldest son, David, join the U.S. Army, and he officiated at the wedding of his oldest daughter, Anita. These were the children he took in as his very own so many years ago and they, along with Samantha and Matthew, knew they were loved.

It is because of people like Gary and Theresa, who in my opinion personify the Tea Party movement, that I become so upset with the liberals playing the race card, as if they had some special insight into the minds and hearts of millions of good and decent Americans.

Not only do their reckless charges of racism devalue the term, and diminish the likelihood of real racist episodes gaining a sympathetic hearing, it impugns the dignity and humanity of some of America's finest people.

Whether it's the elderly woman at her very first protest, the pony-tailed, goateed small business owner, or the devoted wife and mother and her God-fearing, truck-driving husband who loved his family, his church and his community, these are the people who built this country and keep it running so we all may benefit.

These are the congregants at the local church, the parents at the ball games, the shoppers at the grocery store, the mothers picking up the children from school, the fathers and mothers coming home after a long work day and a seemingly longer commute.

These are the people who come to mind when terms like "heartland" and "flyover country" are used.

In fact, the "heartland" and "flyover country" aren't geographical locations but a state of mind, a place of time-honored values that harkens back to the intent of our Founding Fathers when they created this great nation.

This place is steeped in what conservative thinker Russell Kirk called "permanent things," those first principles which transcend generations and are as relevant in the 21st century as they were in the first.

This place is where faith, family, friends and country are revered and selflessness is a personal and voluntary act of love taken by individuals acting alone or collectively on behalf of their neighbors.

This place is where government protects and serves the people rather than impose its will.

This place is where we embrace the dignity and worth of every human being because they are God's creation and we are all precious in His sight.

This place is where humility and service take precedence over arrogance and self-fulfillment.

It's people like these who I've loved and who have loved me, unconditionally. The color of my skin is as far from their minds as the east is from the west.

It is their faith that all hard-working people can thrive in America if given the liberty and opportunity that lives at the heart of the Tea Party movement.

If you want to see for yourself whether or not the Tea Party movement is racist, there's only one way to do it. Go to a Tea Party rally. If you aren't there to disrupt or agitate, we'll welcome you warmly and invite you to observe.

To all Americans who believe in individual liberty, personal responsibility, fiscal accountability and transparency, less intrusive government, and a greater reliance on family, faith and community over government, you have nothing to fear from us. There is no racial, gender or ethnic litmus test, and in these times of dramatic change, we need you.

-15-

Where Do We Go from Here?

"I am not what happened to me;
I am what I choose to become."
~ Carl Jung

Being the political junkie I am, I stayed up late on Election Day 2008 to see history being made. America was going to elect either its first black president or its first female vice president, and the prevailing opinion was that the former would be the case.

In the early morning hours after the election had been decided, a crowd of several thousand gathered at Grant Park in Chicago to celebrate President-elect Barack Obama, who arrived to deliver his victory speech.

The speech wasn't what stood out for me as I watched the scene unfold on television. A little while prior to President-elect Obama's arrival, Fox News had just called the election for Obama. One of the political pundits on duty that night, a seasoned black journalist named Juan Williams, was struggling to contain his emotions as he described the historic event that had just occurred.

Later that evening, as the camera scanned the crowd at Grant Park before Obama's victory speech, I noticed the Rev. Jesse Jackson who, just a few short months before angrily threatened to "cut [Obama's] nuts off" because he felt Obama was talking down to black people on the issue of fatherhood, and he was weeping. Oprah Winfrey was also in the crowd and she, too, was in tears.

I knew these weren't the normal tears of joy shed by the supporters of a victorious candidate, especially coming from Jackson. You could see in his face the release of decades of pain and struggle, and although I agree with almost nothing the man says or does, I was touched by his emotion.

Despite what he has become, he was there at Selma and marched to Montgomery, and he was in Memphis when Dr. King was gunned down, standing just feet below him in the parking lot. He probably never dreamed a black man would become president in his lifetime, and I'm sure that feeling was reinforced by his own two unsuccessful bids for the office.

As moved as I was by his tears, I was disturbed that my own emotions were somewhat muted. I was watching history unfold and an invisible wall breached after more than 400 years, and it should have elicited a strong emotional response from me. What I felt was disappointment—the person I voted for didn't win.

Looking back on it, I realized the reason I didn't react as perhaps some others did is because I evaluated Obama not as a black man, but simply a man. In the immortal words of Dr. King, I was judging him not by the color of his skin but by the content of his character.

I suspect that's not how my black brothers and sisters would see it. To them, the need for black solidarity hasn't gone away and this historic milestone is not an end, but just another marker, albeit a significant one, on the road to racial equality.

Many years ago, Justice Thurgood Marshall, the first black to serve on the U.S. Supreme Court, made a statement that has always stayed with me, and I'm quoting from memory since I've never found it anywhere other than the newspaper I was reading that day:

There is still no place in America where I have to hold my hand in front of my face to know I'm black.

This great and accomplished man woke up every morning with his blackness demanding center stage, because society wouldn't allow him to define himself as anything other than a black man.

In some respects, however, by adopting race as the foundation of our identity as we have done, we are validating society's definition of who we are. I don't see why we need to give society that power over us.

Unlike Justice Marshall, until I became a minor public figure, I could generally go about my daily business without race at the forefront of my consciousness. The people with whom I interacted regularly didn't impose race on me and I didn't make it the center of my life. I was comfortable in my relationships and my friends and acquaintances were comfortable with me.

Since I joined the Bush Administration in 2001 and raised my profile, however, I haven't always been able to avoid the topic of race, and seeking elected office has only made it more prevalent as an issue, although not one of my making.

Some of my black friends take me to task for "avoiding" the issue of race, and tell me I'm oblivious to all the racism swirling around me. I ask them, "If it wasn't disruptive enough for me to notice it, then should it matter to me?"

To them, it should, because it's not all about me and I get that. I know racism exists, I know some people experience it, and I know it has been a hindering factor in their ascendancy. As I've recounted, my exposure to racism has been infrequent and random, and it hasn't posed a barrier to me.

My thinking is that perhaps there is something in my approach to people or circumstances that neutralizes all but the most virulent, unrepentant racists. My desire is to share my approach and experiences with others in the hope they, too, can reach a point where race isn't a barrier in their lives. My goal has always been to live a life free of race, and I do everything I can within my control to achieve it.

It frustrates me when people are critical of me for striving to live a post-racial life. I encounter some blacks who genuinely dislike my color-blind worldview, and accuse me of disowning my black culture and history.

On the contrary, I'm quite interested in my culture and history, especially since I dabble in genealogy as a hobby, and I embrace them as significant determinants of who I am.

My blackness isn't all I think about. It's not the first thing on my mind or even the second or third.

You'd think there was a law against black people placing anything before race as the primary defining factor in their lives. I think it's yet another example of the black community's collectivist worldview at work, a worldview which demands conformity of thought and action to earn acceptance.

Those who object to my worldview are entitled to their opinions, but they can't superimpose their lives over mine. I don't presume to know what they've been through or how it has shaped them, and I try to be respectful of their experiences but, on this particular issue, I'm not offered the same courtesy. It's almost as if they're afraid to validate my conclusions for fear it would delegitimize their grievances.

As I reflect on Justice Marshall's words, I believe my generation and all that follow are very fortunate to live in these times when we consider what he and others of his generation, and generations past, endured to smooth the path for us.

Beginning with the *Brown v. Board of Education* decision, for which Marshall was one of the winning attorneys, our grandparents and parents hacked through the tangle and underbrush of institutionalized discrimination that sought to separate black from white, and cleared a path for us to come together. In doing so, we learned much about our shared dreams and aspirations, and not only did legal barriers fall, so did cultural and relational ones.

Black music is probably the dominant music in American popular culture, and even in my rural county, I see white boys emulating the talk, walk and dress of their black friends. Black music is booming from the car radios of white teenagers as well as black, and interracial dating doesn't cause today's generation to even bat an eye.

Remember when the characters Tom and Helen, the husband and wife in the situation comedy *The Jeffersons*, were considered groundbreaking as the first interracial couple to appear on prime time television? Nowadays, interracial relationships, whether portrayed on television or seen in real life, don't even move the needle on the outrage meter.

Hit shows like *ER*, *Grey's Anatomy*, *CSI*, *Lost*, *Will and Grace*, and *Friends*, just to name a few, have featured black/white interracial couples. Interracial dating and marriage among entertainers is commonplace. I don't know if art is imitating life or influencing it, but what I see at my children's high school is also what I see on television.

Of course, the most telling sign of the progress we've made is that we have a black man as president of the United States, an accomplishment that wouldn't have been possible if he hadn't drawn more of the white vote than any of his Democratic predecessors since Lyndon Johnson in 1964.

In fact, 54% of white people ages 18-29 voted for President Obama and the white vote that put him in power shocked many black observers, inspiring writer Ta-Nehisi Coates to exclaim, "Those of us who overestimated racism would be smart to think about why we were so wrong."

Some, like renowned columnist William Raspberry, recognized the signs that foretold President Obama's election. He wrote in 2005, "Maybe we haven't laid racism to rest, but we have reached the point where what we do matters more than what is done to us. That's great, good news."[38]

In 2004, the Pew Research Center for the People and the Press concluded, "On most issues relating to race, the gap in opinion between white and black Americans remains substantial."[39] As recently as 2007, Pew reported a significant gap between blacks and whites in their perception of racial progress in America, finding "blacks less upbeat about the state of black progress now than at any time since 1983."[40]

This year, however, Pew released a poll on racial attitudes that revealed a dramatic change in the nation's views. It indicates that 70% of white Americans and 60% of black Americans "believe values held by blacks and whites have become more similar in the past decade."[41]

It also says that 65% of whites and 56% of blacks believe the gap between standards of living for the two races has narrowed over the last 10 years.

Thirty-nine percent of black Americans say the "situation for blacks in the U.S." is better than it was five years earlier. That is nearly twice the 20% of blacks who gave the same answer in Pew's 2007 poll.

Fifty-three percent of black Americans also say they expect life in the future to be even better for black people, compared to 41% in 2007.

Fifty-two percent of blacks say that black people who are not getting ahead today are "responsible for their own situation." Only a third of black Americans attributed the plight of black poor people to racism.

As black journalist Juan Williams wrote:

These astounding findings in the Pew poll open a different racial discussion in America. In the past, the big news out of polls of the two races predict-ably showed that white people thought one way and black people thought another. Now here is a poll that finds black and white people finding common ground as never before.[42]

According to Williams, the results of the poll "signaled a new era in American race relations" and he chided the mainstream news media in a Martin Luther King Day editorial for virtually ignoring the poll, declaring they "only see racial division as newsworthy."

A continued discordant note in the midst of this good news, however, is the persistent struggle of urban blacks with poor education, joblessness, poverty, and crime, but even their plight might not be the result of racism, according to black economist Thomas Sowell.

In his book, *Black Rednecks and White Liberals,* Sowell postulates that the urban black culture is a direct derivative of the culture of the Deep South.

According to Sowell, the Deep South in colonial times was populated largely by "people who were called 'rednecks' and 'crackers' in Britain before they ever saw America." From these immigrants came the speech, behavior, aggressiveness and disdain for education that comprises the culture of the Deep South. Remember, for example, George Wallace railing against "pointy-headed intellectuals"? So while millions of blacks migrated to the North in the early-to-mid 20th century, they retained the culture of the region from which they came.

William Raspberry notes Sowell's thesis in his comments on the book:

The redneck culture has been a developmental millstone for both blacks and whites imbued with it—witness the lower academic achievement in the Deep South. But he says it has been preserved most faithfully in the black ghettos...

An intriguing thought, isn't it? If race were the primary determining factor in the problems of poor blacks, then one would expect to see poverty more widespread throughout the black community. Raspberry, again citing Sowell, states:

> *But as Sowell argues—and has been arguing for decades—the racism explanation cannot account for differential outcomes among blacks from within and without the redneck culture. For instance, a recent study found that most of Harvard's black alumni were either from the Caribbean or Africa or were children of Caribbean or African immigrants.*

The bottom line is that too many of us have succeeded in America—we own our own businesses, serve in advanced professions like medicine or the law, lead troops into battle, and occupy the corner office or, in Barack Obama's case, the Oval Office.

Add to that the educational and economic achievements of Caribbean and African blacks who've immigrated to America, and Sowell's theory of culture rather than race being the determining factor in our success or failure makes perfect sense to me.

Of course, Obama's ascension to arguably the most powerful position on the planet is a source of worry for many in the black orthodoxy precisely because it gives validity to the changing perceptions I've addressed.

Anything that diminishes or negates racism as a central cause of social pathologies within the black community is viewed as a threat rather than a sign of progress. The question is who or what is threatened, and why it is important to some to uphold the bogeyman of racism in perpetuity.

The fear among the "race pushers" was that Obama's election would lead too many people (read: white people) to conclude that racism was no longer an insurmountable barrier to black success. What would they then use to exact tribute from white society? What would be their source of power and influence?

Well, isn't eliminating racism as a barrier the end goal of our more than four centuries of struggle? Isn't our desire to be seen not as black, but as human, as equal heirs to the Kingdom?

Raina Kelley, a columnist for *Newsweek*, wrote a poignant letter to her infant son on the occasion of Obama's election and it captures beautifully the hope of a brighter future for black children because of America's victory over its past. She exulted, "With Obama's election, I can mean it when I tell you that the world is available to you."[43]

Kelley declared that we can no longer fall back on the argument of blacks as victims of racism to explain our lack of success. She challenged blacks who become an anchor to those of us who work hard and discipline ourselves to achieve greatness. This attitude reflects a noteworthy change in how we perceive ourselves and the world around us.

Of course, the race pushers have seized upon every opportunity they could since President Obama took office to portray any criticism directed toward him as racism, and they've been aided by left-wing politicians and media for whom such an incendiary charge provides cover for a president who is pushing hard to enact a radical agenda they favor.

What they may not have expected, however, is the pushback from those being accused of racism. Tired of their motives and actions being distorted into a race issue, much of the white public opposing Obama rejects these attempts to label them and appear unlikely to back down.

White guilt is increasingly less potent as a weapon for the race pushers, because fewer whites are willing to tolerate such incitement without evidence of actual wrongdoing, and they refuse to carry the burden of their ancestors.

Even President Obama has come under criticism from the Congressional Black Caucus and other black activists for not doing enough for black people. I found their criticisms intriguing because they clearly expected a black president would cater more to their demands than others, in my opinion an unrealistic expectation of the president of the United States. President Obama himself addressed the folly of such an expectation as he defended himself:

> *The only thing I cannot do is, by law, I cannot pass laws that say "I'm just helping black folks." I'm the president of the entire United States. What I can do is make sure that I am passing laws that help all people, particularly those who are most vulnerable and most in need. That in turn is going to help lift up the African-American community.*

What surprised me most, however, was the public reaction to the caucus' comments. I read through several articles on this episode at a variety of websites, and the comments were overwhelmingly negative and harsh, and that included comments from blacks as well as whites. One black respondent who posted her comments at the Black Voices website essentially captured the essence of most of the comments I read, regardless of the writer's racial background:

> *I am so tired of folks expecting so much when they bring nothing to the table. If you are bringing your "A" game and continue to experience closed doors, that is the time to protest.*

A black man responded to her comments in the affirmative:

I complete (sic) agree with your comments! I'm so tired of these balck (sic) folks coming here online attacking the President, but are in fact doing absolutely nothing except running their mouths as per usual! I have to also agree that black people, both BM and BW need to be more responsible! And, stop always wanting more hand outs! When are we going to finally wake up as a people? Appears like never!

I'm not a sociologist nor do I have detailed polling results or research at my disposal, but my intuition tells me that, while we will continue to have racial episodes, and enclaves where the disparities between black and white are great, the mainstream is anxious for a new dialogue between the races.

So we're at a crossroads. We can't continue with the same race-centered arguments of the past; they ring hollow in President Obama's America.

The warlords of the civil rights era are losing their troops, especially the younger generations, who are told what blacks in America cannot do, yet they see accomplished people splashed on their television and computer screens who look just like them, and one of them is actually in charge of the entire nation. The old arguments aren't being accepted without question anymore.

If we examine the current circumstances of those in the black community who suffer the most, the poor or urban blacks in America, we can conclude our dependence on government since the mid-1960s to combat poverty hasn't yielded results. I believe this is because government approaches poverty as solely a systemic problem rather than a social problem.

Research shows that people who stay out of trouble, get at least a high school diploma, get and keep a job, marry and then have children *in that order* are much less likely to be poor.

These are behavioral steps and not likely to be affected through government policy. In fact, much of government policy toward the poor has discouraged the behaviors that contribute most to poverty reduction.

Just because government has failed, doesn't mean there aren't answers out there.

From a policy perspective, I think we agree that education is the key to advancing the black community, specifically urban blacks and those living in poverty. We need to break away, however, from the tired answers of the past.

We have ample evidence that charter schools, vouchers for private schools, and other parental choice options result in dramatic improvements in reading, writing and math skills, test scores, and graduation rates for black students in some of the worst school districts in the nation.

Black leaders and elected officials are beginning to come around to the benefits of parental choice in the black community. Black Democrats in Washington, DC and New Orleans led the establishment of charter schools and voucher programs for low-income children to attend private schools.

A quick Google survey of parental choice leaders across the country reveals many black faces, some of whom are among the most prominent advocates for parental choice in the nation.

Kevin Chavous of Washington, DC, one of the pre-eminent parental choice leaders in America, is blunt in his assessment of our current public education system and the need for choice to give parents and their children options and hope for the future:

My visits to schools and growing understanding of the realities of public education led me to one stark conclusion: That our current system is not just dysfunctional, it is utterly broken. Yes, many parts excel. Many of its teachers and professionals are deeply committed. But as a system, public education is not working in America...

Unfortunately, our traditional public education system will never reform itself internally. No monopoly ever has. True reform will only take place through external pressure. The most effective form of external pressure comes by way of parental choice...

One approach no longer works with children. Just as diversity of population is one of the greatest strengths of this country, diversity of educational options and experience will help start meaningful change in public education.[44]

It should anger black Americans that, for decades, government at all levels has denied black parents and their children the opportunity to pursue a quality education at the school of their choice, all in the name of politics. Generations of young black people, especially our boys, are condemned to lives of desperation and hopelessness.

Some have called parental choice "the civil rights issue of our time" and we need to understand that the public school bureaucracy, for reasons they need to explain, is standing in the way of our giving our children options *today*. We must not lose another generation of black children; we must form alliances across party lines and ideologies with the singular purpose of saving our children.

On this issue, the first black president is in some respects trailblazing and, in one particularly egregious case, confounding.

He has come out in support of lifting state caps on charter schools and implementing merit pay for teachers, positions that put him at odds with the teachers' unions, their statements to the contrary notwithstanding. On charter schools, he touted his longtime support for these "laboratories of innovation":

> *That leads me to the fourth part of America's education strategy—promoting innovation and excellence in America's schools. One of the places where much of that innovation occurs is in our most effective charter schools. These are public schools founded by parents, teachers, and civic or community organizations with broad leeway to innovate—schools I supported as a state legislator and United States senator.*[45]

He also indicated in his first major address as president on education policy that the primary standard by which he would measure the success of education programs was not ideology, but effectiveness:

> *[We]... will use only one test when deciding what ideas to support with your precious tax dollars. It's not whether an idea is liberal or conservative, but whether it works.*

Yet this same president, his secretary of Education, and their allies in Congress, including non-voting DC Delegate Eleanor Holmes Norton, a black Democrat, have essentially killed the DC Opportunity Scholarship Program by refusing to fund it going forward. Their actions prompted Mr. Chavous and former Washington, DC Mayor Anthony Williams, another black Democrat, to question the credibility of their commitment to the children's education:

> *These naysayers—many of whom are fellow Democrats—see vouchers as a tool to destroy the public education system. Their rhetoric and ire are largely fueled by those special-interest groups that*

*are more dedicated to the adults working in the
education system than to making certain every
child is properly educated...*

*But unless we are willing to embrace all legiti-
mate means to educate our children, we are aban-
doning them. How many more have to go without
a proper education and give up their dreams
before we say, "Enough"?*[46]

The cynic in me suggests the sacrifice of the DC
voucher program was the price Obama had to pay to
buy the teachers' unions' silence on charter schools
and merit pay.

His general contempt for the private sector may be
another factor in his decision. Whatever the reason, the
poor people in Washington for whom he swears he's
fighting every day have ample reason to believe it's all
just talk. He took away a program the parents wanted,
which even his own Department of Education said was
working, and forced them to remain in the educational
prison from which they had hoped to emerge.

Mr. Chavous, a black Democrat and a supporter of
President Obama, remains eloquent and passionate in
his defense of parental choice:

*Choice as a concept seems simple enough: As a
parent, you know the most and care the most about
your child, and education is an indisputable part of
a child's rearing. A parent ought to have the ability
to make the best decision for their child's future.*

*We are blessed with a strong public school
system in the United States and in most cases our
children receive a splendid education, but we all
know that right now many children in our country
are trapped in failing schools. They cannot wait
for another study, another task force or more
excuses. Nor are huge taxes [sic] increases and*

higher appropriations the Answer, as many of the nation's worst school districts are also the best funded. These children need help now. Their future depends on it.

Parental choice sometimes means different solutions in different states. It is important, however, for more viable educational options to exist to break the mold of our one-size-fits-all approach.[47]

That leads me to perhaps the most challenging suggestion of all in regard to moving us forward. Unless we have aspirations of moving to Africa or creating our own reservations, we are Americans and, as committed as we are to equal justice, we must be equally committed to reconciliation with the nation we call home.

That will require us to embrace the culture that makes America unique while still keeping our sense of identity which sustained us through the dark times in America's past. We must adopt the American ethos and make it our own.

First, we must learn to celebrate the unique and unrepeatable individuals that make up the black community, and society, as a whole. This is not the shallow, superficial diversity of race, gender, ethnicity or sexual orientation touted by liberals. We need to break out of our collectivist culture if we are to exceed poverty and mediocrity, and strive toward excellence.

Individual liberty and responsibility are fundamental traits in the American psyche and sociologist Shelby Steele describes them well:

Here is a brief litany of obvious truths that have been resisted in the public discourse of black America over the last thirty years: a group is no stronger than its individuals; when individuals transform themselves they transform the group; the freer the individual, the stronger the group;

*social responsibility begins in individual respon-
sibility. Add to this an indisputable fact that has
also been unmentionable: that American greatness has a lot to do with a culturally ingrained
individualism, with the respect and freedom historically granted individuals to pursue their happiness—this despite many egregious lapses and
an outright commitment to the oppression of black
individuals for centuries. And there is one last
obvious but unassimilated fact: ethnic groups that
have asked a lot from their individuals have done
exceptionally well in America even while enduring
discrimination.*[48]

Indeed we banded together because we had to, but
most of us didn't realize our freedom to be individuals—
to be a unique man or a woman.

Black artists and intellectuals who emigrated from
the U.S. to France in the 1950s and 1960s were energized by the freedom to live as individuals and this
freedom stimulated their creativity and contributed to
their greatest works.

I liberated myself from being defined as part of a collective, not only by whites but also by blacks.

In the past, blacks banded together out of necessity,
but we figured out that we could use collective thought
and action against a 'guilty' white population to get our
way. As a result, blacks have not been kind to those of
their own race who broke away and established their
individual identities.

I contend that the collective model of behavior is destined to fail because it doesn't unleash the full potential
of the black community.

Black groupthink is also doomed because white guilt
over past iniquities is diminishing with the passage of
time.

Therefore, I would encourage us to reject collectivism and embrace the individual worth and dignity of every person. Fully accomplished individuals result in a blossoming and vibrant race, and individual liberty aligns us with one of the intrinsic characteristics of being an American.

Another aspect of America's national character, one that is closely related to individual liberty, is free enterprise. If individual liberty is the exercise of free minds, free enterprise is the exercise of free markets. It is free enterprise that the Declaration of Independence describes as "the pursuit of happiness."

In April 2010, I attended a speech by the same Arthur C. Brooks cited earlier, president of the American Enterprise Institute. He declared, "Free enterprise is not simply an economic alternative; it is central to the American experience." He also said American culture is different from that of any other nation because of its orientation toward the free enterprise system.

Professor Brooks, a social scientist, came armed with data to support his position. A Pew Research poll indicated that 70% of Americans support free enterprise despite the severe ups and downs of the economy. A similar Gallup Poll puts the figure at 85%. He cited several studies that reveal most Americans want lower taxes and less intrusion of government in the private sector, and they prefer the opportunity to create wealth over the redistribution of wealth.

He went on to say we need to reclaim the moral high ground when defending free enterprise, because it is the difference between flourishing and floundering for human beings. It is the fairest system because it rewards hard work and excellence, and gives the most humans opportunities to flourish.

It also richly contributes to happiness because it encourages earned success. Whether it's lottery winnings, inherited money, welfare checks or government grants, studies show that recipients of unearned success are less happy than those who have pursued their happiness and achieved it by their own labors.

Brooks' argument that free enterprise is a mainstream value, maximizes the potential for earthly happiness, and is morally superior to any other economic system, resonated strongly with me. I have long advocated that free enterprise creates the most jobs, reduces poverty, and enhances human dignity and happiness by freeing us to achieve as much as our skills, knowledge and work ethic allow.

Jobs programs that come out of Washington generally don't create nearly enough opportunities for those who want to work, because the focus tends to be on government jobs (i.e., teachers, public safety officials, correctional officers) and public infrastructure work that ends as soon as the project concludes.

Moreover, government jobs are not created unless there is a robust private sector behind them. Not a penny paid in salary to government workers was created by government, but rather the blood, toil, tears and sweat of hard-working Americans. Government cannot create wealth, only confiscate and redistribute it.

Yet government jobs are increasing in record numbers, while private sector hiring has been flat for about the past decade and has fallen precipitously in recent years. This is an unsustainable employment model. To quote former British Prime Minister Margaret Thatcher, "[E]ventually you run out of other people's money."

As *Washington Post* writer Alec MacGillis wrote, "Standing apart from the back-and-forth has been an unavoidable fact: No program has helped lift up the poor in recent years as much as a strong economy."[49]

History has demonstrated time and again that wealth creation, the unique province of free enterprise, is what works best to reduce the numbers of poor people.

We need to move from being employees to becoming business owners and employers ourselves. Entrepreneurship is the most effective and enduring approach to generating wealth within the black community, and creating a generation of achievers to shake off the pathologies and dependencies of the past.

The most effective poverty reduction initiatives in developing nations are not large-scale international aid programs, but micro loans which have encouraged entrepreneurship, and allowed people to generate income, build wealth and break out of poverty.

If micro loans can bring people in developing nations out of poverty and into the freedom of generating their own income and building generational wealth for themselves and their families, why can't they work in our urban areas where poor blacks are concentrated? I believe they can—if we develop an entrepreneurial spirit within the urban black community.

We need to emulate recent immigrants to America, who have become the most active entrepreneurs in our urban areas. African, Asian (including Indian) and Hispanic owned businesses are revitalizing our cities.

In 2000, the U.S. Census showed that while immigrants make up 36% of New York City's population, they comprise 49% of the city's self-employed. In 2005, at least 22 of Los Angeles' 100 fastest growing companies were established by first-generation immigrants.

The Schomburg Center for Research in Black Culture observed a strong entrepreneurial spirit and its positive results within America's African immigrant community:

This entrepreneurial spirit is deeply ingrained in Africa, where the informal economic sector is particularly dynamic. To be one's own boss is a common aspiration there, and Africans in the United States make the most of the opportunities offered by a free market economy. These entrepreneurs do not look for a job; they come to create one. From infor-mation technology to the oil industry, they have established several successful companies.

They are also a major force in the revitalization of some inner-city neighborhoods. Without help from banks, using their own money augmented by income from communal rotating savings funds, they have opened stores, car services, and restaurants that provide needed services to the community.[50]

Black community activists and churches, in col-laboration with the private, non-profit and public sec-tors, should facilitate the training and development of aspiring entrepreneurs, and help them obtain the start-up capital necessary to establish their own businesses. As with education, alliances formed around a common goal can cut across political parties and ideologies, and advance the cause of reducing poverty in the black community.

At the risk of sounding cynical, poverty will never disappear altogether because poverty is a natural occur-rence in a fallen world.

Even Jesus said, "The poor you will always have with you..."[am] Yes, Jesus also expects us, specifically Christians, to do everything in our power to help the poor, but He offered no illusions about eradicating poverty.

Poverty isn't just a matter of finding the right solu-tions. No solution can bring about the life change that motivates people to work their way out of their circum-stances. The will—that "want to"—has to come from within.

As we fully adopt the American ethos into the black community, acknowledging the inherent dignity and worth of the individual and the human potential

---

[am] Matthew 26:11.

unleashed by free enterprise, we can come closer to achieving the other goal that leads to greater racial harmony: forgiveness.

Forgiveness is hard. It means truly releasing the pain of the past and never reclaiming it. It means loving those who once were and, may still be, your enemies. It means, as Jesus says:

> *For if you love those who love you, what reward do you have? Do not even the tax collectors do the same? If you greet only your brothers, what more are you doing than others? Do not even the Gentiles do the same? Therefore you are to be perfect, as your heavenly Father is perfect.*[an]

Forgiveness is an unconditional act. It doesn't seek adulation, nor does it wish judgment upon one's foes. It doesn't justify the wrongs of the past, but it clears the path to the present and future.

Most importantly, forgiveness doesn't look back. The past can be an anchor if we allow it to find a foothold in our minds and hearts. After all, the past cannot be changed and there is no practical application of the past to our present circumstances other than as a warning or a lesson to be learned.

There is no objective scale or measure that can calculate the value of past wrongs, so there is no way to fully compensate for them. The best solution is to forgive the debt and press ahead.

My faith helps me to understand true forgiveness. We could never perform enough good deeds or show enough contrition to fully cleanse ourselves of sin. Therefore, Christ made the ultimate sacrifice to redeem us.

[an] Matthew 5:46-48.

He said, "For I will be merciful to their iniquities, and I will remember their sins no more."[ao] Of course, God knows everything and is not erasing our sins from His divine memory. His commitment to us is that He will receive us as if He has no memory of our sins: "As far as the east is from the west, So far has He removed our transgressions from us."[ap]

That kind of mercy, even if directed at those who do not believe they've done anything for which they require it, is potent. It frees blacks and whites from centuries of baggage based on race and it gives us an opportunity to move forward together with hope.

St. Paul says, "There is neither Jew nor Greek, there is neither slave nor free man, there is neither male nor female; for you are all one in Christ Jesus."[aq]

I don't diminish the more than 400 years of racial struggle between blacks and whites in America, but I refuse to be imprisoned by history. If policies and attitudes based on racial resentment and perpetual victimhood aren't working, why not try something different? It's time for us to begin anew and write a fresh story to replace the old, tired one that leads to nowhere. Embracing, not damning America, clears the way for whites and blacks to be equal partners in liberty and prosperity. Forgiveness, not retribution, is where genuine and lasting racial reconciliation lives. I've been blessed to live there most of my life—won't you join me?

[ap] Hebrews 8:12.

[ap] Psalm 103:12.

[aq] Galatians 3:28.

Endnotes

1 Lila Rose, "Abortions earmarked by race: An investigation of Planned Parenthood's money," *The Advocate*, Winter 2008, p. 3, (http://www.laadvocate.com/Advocate3.pdf). Audio recordings available at Live Action's Planned Parenthood Racism Project, http://liveaction.org/index.php/projects/racism.

2 Nadine Brozan, "Another Sanger Leads Planned Parenthood," *The New York Times*, January 23, 1991, (http://www.nytimes.com/1991/01/23/nyregion/another-sanger-leads-planned-parenthood.html).

3 Ibid.

4 Ryan Rizza, "The Abortion Capital of America," *New York Magazine,* Dec. 4, 2005, http://nymag.com/nymetro/news/features/15248/.

5 Reverend Al Sharpton, speech at NARAL Pro-Choice America Dinner, Washington, DC, January 21, 2003. (Transcript © 2003 Eric M. Appleman, Democracy in Action, http://www.gwu.edu/~action/2004/interestg/naral012103/sharp012103spt.html).

[6] The Journal of Blacks in Higher Education, "There Is a Wide Discrepancy Among the States in High School Graduation Rates for Black Male Students," August 28, 2008, http://www.jbhe.com/latest/index082108.html.

[7] Ibid.

[8] Christopher B. Swanson, Ph.D., *Cities in Crisis: A Special Analytical Report on High School Graduation*, published by EPE Research Center, Bethesda, MD, (http://www.americaspromise.org/~/media/Files/Our%20Work/Dropout%20Prevention/Cities%20in%20Crisis/Cities In Crisis Report 2008.ashx), April 1, 2008, p. 9.

[9] John Robert, Warren, Ph.D., University of Minnesota, *Graduation Rates for Choice and Public School Students in Milwaukee, 2003-2007*, published by School Choice Wisconsin, Milwaukee, WI, (http://www.schoolchoicewi.org/currdev/detail.cfm?id=271), May 2007, p. 7.

[10] Knowledge Is Power Program, FAQ, http://www.kipp.org/faq, June 12, 2010.

[11] Chesapeake Science Point Public Charter School, Hanover, MD, (http://www.mycsp.org/documents/CSP MSA Press Release July 23 2008.pdf), Press Release July 23, 2008.

[12] "What Are ...Maryland Public Charter Schools?" 2007-08 Fact Sheet published by Maryland Charter School Network, Baltimore, MD, http://www.mdcharternetwork.org/documents/FactSheet-1007-final.pdf.

[13] "DC School Choice Leaders Blast Appropriators' Decision to Kill School Voucher Program: Call on Obama and Durbin to Stand With DC's Low-Income Families," the Heartland Institute, Chicago, IL, (http://www.heartland.org/full/26506/DC_School_Choice_Leaders_Blast_Appropriators_Decision_to_Kill_School_Voucher_Program.html), 12/10/2009.

[14] Jim Waters, "Blacks' Support for School Choice Increases in New Orleans, Nationwide," published by the Heartland Institute in *School Reform News*, September 2008 (http://www.heartland.org/infotech-news.org/article/23744/Blacks_Support_for_School_Choice_Increases_in_New_Orleans_Nationwide.html).

[15] The Heartland Institute, "DC School Choice Leaders Blast Appropriators' Decision to Kill School Voucher Program."

[16] Waters.

[17] Jesse Jackson, "How we respect life is the over-riding moral issue," Right to Life News, January, 1977, (republished at http://groups.csail.mit.edu/mac/users/rauch/nvp/consistent/jackson.html).

[18] Carl M. Cannon, "Abortion, Eugenics and the Meaning of Margaret Sanger," Politics Daily, http://www.politicsdaily.com/2009/07/22/ginsburgs-remark-stirs-an-old-debate-abortion-eugenics-and-th/, 07/22/09.

[19] Spengler, "The peculiar theology of black liberation," Asia Times, http://www.atimes.com/atimes/Front_Page/JC18Aa01.html, March 18, 2008.

[20] Crystal K. Roberts, "Nationally-syndicated columnist, William Raspberry, shares 30-plus years of widsom in the workplace," *Black Collegian*, (http://findarticles.com/p/articles/mi_qa3628/is_199910/ai_n8867025/?tag=content;col1), Oct. 1999.

[21] Lisa Miller, "Finding His Faith," *Newsweek*, (http://www.newsweek.com/2008/07/11/finding-his-faith.html), July 12, 2008.

[22] Roberta Green Ahmanson, Julie Ryan and Cherise Ryan, "Into the arms of God," *World Magazine*, (http://www.worldmag.com/articles/13536), November 24, 2007.

[23] Rick Boxx, "A Modern-Day Workplace Tragedy," Monday Manna Devotional published 14 Jan 2008 by CBMC International, http://www.cbmcint.org/resources/monday_manna?manna_id=1198.

[24] Digital Publius, "Of Toms and Sambos," http://web.me.com/toddgroup/digital_publius/Blog/Entries/2009/8/26_Of_Toms_and_Sambos.html, Wednesday, August 26, 2009.

[25] Digital Publius, "The Voters Stupid," http://web.me.com/toddgroup/digital_publius/Blog/Entries/2009/11/24_The_Voters_Stupid.html, Tuesday, November 24, 2009.

[26] Ibid.

[27] barackobama.com, Barack Obama Addresses Planned Parenthood, (http://www.youtube.com/watch?v=uUl99id2SvM), 7/17/07, posted January 23, 2008.

[28] James Sherley, "True Liberty and Justice for All Ages," Spero News, http://www.speroforum.com/site/article.asp?idCategory=34&idsub=127&id=15623&t=True+Liberty+and+Justice+for+All+Ages, Friday, July 4, 2008.

[29] Nicholas Kralev, "Rice hits U.S. 'birth defect,'" *The Washington Times*, March 28, 2008, (no longer available online, June 11, 2010).

[30] Eamon Javers, "Obama: It's (mostly) not about race," *Politico* (http://www.politico.com/news/stories/0909/27330.html), September 19, 2010.

[31] Javers, citing President Obama to CNN's John King, host of *State of the Union*.

[32] Javers, citing President Obama to David Gregory of NBC's *Meet the Press*.

[33] Javers, citing President Obama to George Stephanopoulos of ABC's *This Week*.

[34] barackobama.com, *President Obama Announces Vote 2010*, (http://www.youtube.com/watch?v=oh-yR1H-WkbM), April 28, 2010.

[35] Hazel Trice Edney, NNPA Editor-in-Chief, "Despite Widespread Appeals, Obama Fails to Appoint Black Woman to Supreme Court," Black Voice News (http://www.blackvoicenews.com/news/news-wire/44391-despite-widespread-appeals-obama-fails-to-appoint-black-woman-to-supreme-court.html), Monday, 10 May 2010.

[36] Ibid.

[37] Ibid.

[38] William Raspberry, "Going Beyond Racism," *The Washington Post*, (http://www.washington-post.com/wp-dyn/content/article/2005/05/15/AR200505150813.html), Monday, May 16, 2005.

[39] The Pew Research Center for the People and the Press, "The 2004 Political Landscape," http://people-press.org/report/?pageid=754, November 5, 2003.

[40] Pew Research Center, "Blacks See Growing Values Gap Between Poor and Middle Class: Optimism about Black Progress Declines," http://pewsocialtrends.org/pubs/700/black-public-opinion, November 13, 2007.

[41] Pew Research Center, "Blacks Upbeat about Black Progress, Prospects: A Year After Obama's Election," http://pewsocialtrends.org/pubs/749/blacks-upbeat-about-black-progress-obama-election, January 12, 2010.

[42] Juan Williams, "Media Ignores Good News About Race," FOXNews.com, http://www.foxnews.com/opinion/2010/01/18/juan-williams-martin-luther-king-blacks-whites-pew-poll/, January 18, 2010.

[43] Raina Kelley, "A Letter to My Son On Election Night," *Newsweek*, (http://www.newsweek.com/2008/11/04/a-letter-to-my-son-on-election-night.html), November 05, 2008.

[44] Kevin P. Chavous, "A Smart Start Strategy for School Reform," http://www.kevinpchavous.com/content/chavouseducationvision.htm, June 14, 2010.

[45] Remarks by the President of the United States to the Hispanic Chamber of Commerce on a Complete and Competitive American Education, White House transcript (http://www.whitehouse.gov/the_press_office/Remarks-of-the-President-to-the-United-States-Hispanic-Chamber-of-Commerce/), March 10, 2009.

[46] Anthony A. Williams and Kevin P. Chavous, "Education, By Any Means" *The Washington Post*, (http://www.washingtonpost.com/wp-dyn/content/article/2009/04/13/AR2009041302027.html), Tuesday, April 14, 2009.

[47] Kevin P. Chavous, Parental Choice Movement, http://www.kevinpchavous.com/content/parentalchoice-movement.htm, June 14, 20110.

[48] Shelby Steele, "The age of white guilt: and the disappearance of the black individual," *Harper's Magazine*, November 30, 1999, (republished by the Center for Individual Rights http://www.cir-usa.org/articles/156.html), June 14, 2010.

[49] Alec MacGillis, "On Poverty, Edwards Faces Old Hurdles: Critics Say He Brings Few Fresh Ideas to Signature Issue," *The Washington Post*, (http://www.washingtonpost.com/wp-dyn/content/article/2007/05/06/AR2007050601322.html), Monday, May 7, 2007.

[50] Schomburg Center for Research in Black Culture, http://www.inmotionaame.org/migrations/topic.cfm?migration=13&topic=5&bhcp=1, June 14, 2010.

Breinigsville, PA USA
24 February 2011
256312BV00001B/2/P